Let's Dish Up a Dinner Party!

A Fab Guide to Entertaining with Style

LET'S DISH UP A DINNER PARTY!

A FAB GUIDE TO ENTERTAINING WITH STYLE

NELSON ASPEN

KENSINGTON BOOKS
www.kensingtonbooks.com

KENSINGTON BOOKS are published by

Kensington Publishing Corp.
850 Third Avenue
New York, NY 10022

ISBN 0-7582-0697-6

First printing: October 2004

10 9 8 7 6 5 4 3 2 1

Printed in the United States of America

To Mother and Dad, my first and best examples
of hospitality and good taste.

To Glenn and all my fab friends,
who continually fill my life with joy and laughter.

To *you*! Why go out when you can stay in
and make every dinner a party?

CONTENTS

Contents

x   Contents

PREFACE

My best friend's Manhattan apartment looks out over Central Park and is perfectly decorated with exquisite mid-century furnishings and art. Even his Siamese cats match the motif. My favorite part of his home, however, is the state-of-the-art stainless steel kitchen. Maddeningly, this chef's paradise is never used except when I blow into town and decide to cook! Oh, sure . . . his catered cocktail parties occur seasonally, but day-to-day home-cooked dinners are more rare than Susan Lucci Emmy wins!

Oddly enough, many of my friends right here in Los Angeles are also strangers to their own kitchens and dining rooms. More than busy schedules and habitual restaurant-hopping, I blame the Food Network for consumer inundation and intimidation! How many times have you watched those wizards of "aahs" on their two-dimensional kitchen sets and shrugged, forlorn, thinking, "I could never do that!"

Well, of course you can't. You don't have a staff of researchers, writers, assistants, technicians, designers, editors, and make-up artists to turn you into an Emeril, Bobby, or Sarah. What you do have, dear hearts, is me.

At least once a month, I dish up a very merry dinner party *chez moi* and all it requires are the components you will find in the pages that follow. And unlike those *Queer Eye* guys (*queer* literally means "suspicious" or "nauseated"—bad qualities for a dinner party) who just want to take your individuality and make it over, I think at-home entertainment should be gay all the way!

Merriam-Webster's Ninth Collegiate Dictionary defines **gay** as follows: "*adj* happily excited, merry; keenly alive and exuberant; having or inducing high spirits—bright, lively; brilliant; given to social pleasures." Now *that's* the way to party!

Oh, yes, it also means "homosexual," but FYI, I am not the wig-wearing, Judy Garland–crooning, rainbow-waving fellow you invariably see featured in your local news coverage of the Pride Parades. I have no body piercings, no pink triangle on my Benz bumper, nor do I snap my fingers and refer to everyone as "girl." Although it's only a fifteen-minute drive to West Hollywood, I much prefer having an assortment of friends under my own roof than being packed into a crowded bar under someone else's.

I do admit, however, to loving to cook and garden, singing a song around the piano, and shopping. I adore my mother, listen to both classical and dance music and, yes, I take excellent care of my skin.

Most of all, I enjoy opening my home to share not only delicious

food and beverages, but conversation, camaraderie, and laughter. I am a professional pundit, but I save my best gossip for those gathered at my dinner table. One can't rely merely on the repast for a successful soiree, it's only one tessera in the larger mosaic. And anyone who's studied biology (or gotten past first base) knows that the way to a man's heart isn't *really* through his stomach!

My mother, Joyce Ann, the right balance of "lady" and "broad," introduced me to the joys of both entertaining and food at an early age. I was a porky kid, but she had the insight to detect an entertainer lurking under all that excess weight and so, took me to audition for a Main Line production of *The House at Pooh Corner.* The cast would be all adults except for three roles. Too fat to be Christopher Robin, I was thrilled to be offered my choice from the other two available children's parts; I wanted to be my favorite character, Roo, in the worst way. Mother gently guided me to accept the supporting lead instead ("Just look, honey, it has so many more *lines!*"), and a porcine thespian was born. I still have a special bias toward Piglet. Tiddly-pom!

Mother used to have guests "sign" the kitchen table by writing their names on a piece of paper while pressing down hard into the soft wood with their pens, so their autographs would be permanently engraved for posterity. I grew up believing that if the kitchen is the heart of one's home, the table is its soul!

My own giant table nearly fills the entire dining room and has been visited by movie stars and masseurs, housewives and haberdashers, circuit queens and circus clowns (strikingly similar at times), aerobics instructors and accountants. Some guests have been as young as four and others as young as eighty. But whomever the guest, I believe they left my parties happy and well-fed—feeling like my little slice of glitzy L.A. is really *home.* Maybe that's why, year after year, friends automatically gravitate to it for holidays and special occasions.

You're going to learn how to accomplish this on your own, whether you hang your hat in a city skyscraper or a country cottage. Here come a plethora of my tips, ideas, and favorite recipes for throwing gay dinner parties. You will also savor more than a few mouthfuls of choice insider Hollywood buzz. I hope this will be the first of endless volumes on the subject because, after all, there are no limits to how creative one can be in sharing the rewards of hospitality.

Have fun! I wish you a lifetime of dinner parties filled with gaiety!

Nelson Aspen

Hollywood, California

Stock the Pantry

Keeping a well-stocked pantry and refrigerator is an important prerequisite not only for dinner parties, but also for quick meals after a long day at the office, unexpected company, or an impromptu brunch. Here are some items you should always be sure to keep on hand.

- Extra virgin olive oil. You can use it in almost every dish and pretty bottles help decorate your shelves.
- Balsamic vinegar. Ditto.
- Assorted pastas
- Bread mix. If you don't already own a bread machine, run out to Williams Sonoma. For a reasonable price that includes a lifetime guarantee, you will never have store-bought bread again!
- Assorted low-fat salad dressings. They make great marinades.

- Salsa
- Worcestershire, soy, and tabasco sauces
- Garlic (cloves or minced)
- Sun-dried tomatoes (tomatoes contain lycopene and beta-carotene to help protect against that So Cal sun damage!)
- Cans of chopped or diced tomatoes. You'll be surprised how often these come in handy and they can help stretch your portions, if need be.
- Cans of chicken broth
- Cans of seasoned and plain bread crumbs
- Jar of capers
- Jars and jars of gorgeous nibblies like stuffed olives, cornichons, and roasted peppers
- Inexpensive wines. Running out during a party can be catastrophic! My faves, Mondavi & Coppola, have great selections ranging from the affordable to pricey. Simple table wines, red and white, always come in handy for cooking, as well.

- Plenty of spices, especially basil, parsley, and cilantro. If you're ambitious, grow an herb garden and you'll never run short. Consider making your own spice/herb blends with the food processor or your best knife. Put them in decorative bottles to display—they'll be prettier, tastier, and fresher than store bought. When it comes to salt and pepper, go for kosher or sea salt and freshly ground black pepper.

In the refrigerator

- Assorted soft drinks and bottled water
- A bottle of good champagne. You never know when there will be a reason to celebrate.

- A selection of cheeses
- Eggs

In the freezer

- Boneless, skinless chicken breasts
- Frozen peas. When in doubt, throw some into almost any dish! My ninety-six-year-old grandmother taught me to eat them like candy.
- Compound butters, which are instant flavorful sauces for steaming hot meats, rice, pastas, or veggies. Blend equal parts cold butter and olive oil with herbs and seasonings of your choice (i.e. garlic, sun-dried tomatoes, black olives, anchovies, rosemary). Roll in parchment paper to form small cylinders, twist the ends, and store in the freezer to keep handy for anytime use. These may also be packed into ramekins and placed on your table to be used as decorative and yummy spreads.
- Freshly ground, or whole, coffee beans
- Ice

With these staples, you'll be pretty much covered even if your handsome husband throws you a curve ball by bringing home the boss. You may want to keep your own list of must-haves, updating and adding to it as experience dictates. My list is always expanding! Still, it's a far cry from the days when I had to rely on the smoke alarm to tell me when the meal was finally *finished*.

"Better is a dinner of vegetables where love is, than a fatted ox and hatred with it."   —PROVERBS, 15:17

SETTING THE STAGE

Even if I don't have a fire blazing in the Batchelder fireplace, I like to make my guests feel instantly at home when they walk through the front door. Be objective and literally step into your home from the outside (see sidebar on page 10 for my thoughts on your outdoor entrance) and ask yourself: What is the atmosphere like in here? What does this home's environment say about the people who live here? Notice the details of the room, the smells, the— dare I say it—*feng shui*!

A very important thing I do is to lock the cat in the back bedroom and put the dog out in the yard (which I, of course, have had cleaned up), even though they both match the decor. FYI, I didn't plan it that way . . . it just happened. This way everybody's happy and fur-free. Close friends will take time to pay the pets a private visit, and no one has to politely pretend they don't notice the Springer spaniel's plaintive face as she drools on their knee at the table, nor brush an Abyssinian's swishing tail away from their dinner plate.

If you don't have pets but you *do* have children, the theory is the same. Get a sitter to entertain them while *you* entertain your guests. One wouldn't/shouldn't subject friends to kids climbing all over them, either. What about roommates? Either include them in your plans or wait until they're out of town to host your party. The latter might work better if you want the evening to have your *signature* on it. I once lived with a well-heeled roommate who segued his prep school education and Ivy League degree into a profitable career as a porn director. I remember at one point coming home to find an impressively built young man pleasuring himself in the spare bathroom while my roommie worked a camera to record every inch of it—an extreme example of the unexpected popping up, and the reason for ending that particular living arrangement. I mean, how could I possibly have guests using that bathroom with King Dong lurking around!?

If your guests are good friends, display photographs of some of your fun times. It's an instant way for them to know how special they are to you. You change your calendar monthly, why not the piccies in your frames?

Worried that your living space is not conducive to entertaining? Pshaw! "Bloom where you're planted," I always say! Skew the direction of your party toward what you have to work with. For instance, if it's a tiny studio apartment, harken back to summer camp or slumber parties and have everyone sit in a circle on the floor. Comfy pillows and candlelight can make an indoor picnic a perfect plan! Another alternative for apartment dwellers is to check with the landlord about taking over an outdoor or common area for the evening. Make sure you plan a menu that's easy to schlep from your kitchen . . . or set up a buffet in your dining room and have everyone meet you after they've piled their plates high.

If you have the storage space, be a party pack-rat and save old movie posters for your Oscar night celebration. Out-of-date campaign banners, buttons, and bumper stickers make great décor for an Election night bash. You get the idea! Let your imagination go wild. Why not print out souvenir menus with catchy course items named for your guests or the occasion? "Claire's Clams Casino" or "Murray's Meringue Pie" will be remembered long after digestion!

As for the following advice, don't assume it's all a given. You may have a lot on your mind, so make a mental or literal checklist.

Select some background music that is familiar but not intrusive. Compilations are best, in case a guest has a distaste for a particular artist. Try throwing a mix of classical, jazz, and new age CDs into the player and for God's sake, keep the volume down.

Candles are great, in all shapes and sizes, especially if they're gifts from some of the very people you have invited. Don't light any with strong scents, and incense is strictly taboo. You don't want anything to interfere with the tempting aromas that emanate from your kitchen. Even if you've lit every wick in the place, keep some electricity on. Unless you're playing Spin the Bottle or telling ghost stories, it's uncomfortable to be entertained in a dark room.

Since the cat is put away, fill up some vases with fresh, seasonal flowers or float some in decorative bowls. Always keep an extra vase on hand in case someone is thoughtful enough to bring you a bouquet. Less is more, remember, so don't get carried away and create a funereal feeling. Filling a bowl with fresh fruit is pretty, too, and is longer lasting and less expensive than flowers.

Make your flowers last longer by cutting the stems at an angle and adding just a few drops of bleach to the water to keep bacteria from forming. Use tepid water—it travels up the stems more rapidly than cold.

Quickly whisk away coats, jackets, and purses so that everyone can nestle into their own uncluttered, ultra comfortable territories. Little niceties mean a lot, so set out plenty of coasters, ashtrays (if you're smoker-friendly), and cocktail napkins.

The greatest courtesy you can extend to yourself and your guests is to have a sparkling clean home. Every time you entertain is an opportunity to rid your home of clutter. I have a special area of the garage set aside for yard sales and Goodwill donations, so when in doubt, move it out! Set aside extra time beforehand for a good housekeeping sweep, or spend some extra money on having a maid service come in. Think how mortified Mrs. So-and-So will be if her hand slips under a sofa cushion and grabs hold of an old pretzel. Being a host and preparing for a dinner party is not too different from being a celebrity getting ready for an important interview. If all the details and dirty work are completed ahead of time, the event itself will be smooth sailing, and you can afford to be gracious and charming without Debra Messing–around!

I once had a partner whose cooking was renowned and friends would gush appreciatively. Envious of the raves heaped upon him, I couldn't help but wonder if these guests also appreciated the cleanliness of my toilet bowls. They might not notice . . . but you can bet they would if those toilets *weren't* immaculate! (A great tip if you have a piano: brighten up those ivories with some white vinegar.) You can bet your sweet bippy that, even if they don't work for the tabloids, some people *will* snoop in your medicine chest or cupboards. You're simply too fascinating to resist!

Even the best dishwashers leave spots. Your dishes, glasses, and silverware should all shine. Double-check each piece when setting the table. This goes for the linens, too. Every napkin should be examined for stains, discoloration, or tears. Grandma's hand-sewn damask tablecloth brought over from the old country won't impress anyone if it has a cigarette burn or traces of last Thanksgiving's gravy. Your table setting should reflect the mood of the party you are throwing. A Mexican fiesta calls for bright colors. Casual conversation might mean mismatched place mats or napkin rings. Try a flashy *fleur de lis* serviette fold if it's a more elegant occasion.

What's that? You don't know how to execute a *fleur de lis* fold?! Never fear, innocent one! My talented designer friend John Tripp, of Sakow and Tripp, spells it out for us. "While seated, position a square napkin in a diamond position in front of you on the table. Fold the top point down to evenly match up with the bottom point. Take both left and right points and fold down so both these points meet with the bottom point. Take what's now become the top point and fold down three inches. Create a 'karate chop' position with your right hand and fold one half of the right half of the napkin, at an angle, underneath. Repeat with the left side of the napkin. Fold back each top fold "wing" and tuck end points of wings back underneath." There! That should edify you folding fanatics! (Don't fret . . . try it a few times and you'll get it.)

Are your silver and china sets short one fork and two bread plates? Got a cracked charger? Check out www.replacementsltd.com, based in North Carolina. They can locate perfect matches of almost any set, no matter how rare or how long out of production. How incredible and effortless it was to find flawless Wedgwood coffee urns, tea cups, and cigarette boxes from the discontinued 1950 Whitehall pattern of Grandfather Aspen!

Unless you've specified a particular attire, wear relaxed, comfortable clothes that are pristine and neat. No jeans or stocking feet. This way, you look "at home," but will coordinate with anyone who shows up either *over-* or *under*dressed. Imagine the pressure I heaped upon myself when Mr. Blackwell came to dine one night! Would I find myself on his annual Worst Dressed List?! I opted at the last minute for a cashmere pullover in a neutral ecru . . . a wise choice. Only my shoes were deemed "been there, done that" by the doyen of design!

Be clean, manicured, coiffed. *The King of Queens* royal star Leah Remini was lightning-fast to notice how well groomed my eyebrows were within seconds of our meeting, believe you me! A simple black blazer works great to throw over and dress up a casual shirt and slacks, fellows. Just be sure not to ever make the mistake I did and advise a blind date, "You'll know me. I'll be in a *black blazer*." He ended up looking for me behind the wheel of an SUV! Another missed opportunity . . .

A dinner party isn't the place to make a fashion statement unless it's a masquerade or Halloween celebration. A certain famous daytime actor showed his true colors when he pulled up to my house on his huge, noisy Harley Davidson. He was proudly clad from head to toe in full leather regalia. I was terrified! He looked so much less scary on *The Young and the Restless* in those tailored designer suits. The only thing I whip is topping!

"Duels, burials, swindlings, affairs of state—everything is a pretext for a good dinner." —JEAN ANOUILH, FRENCH PLAYWRIGHT (1910– 1987)

Of course you will rave about any gifts you're brought, but the best way to ensure you receive something you truly adore is to be a seasoned gift *giver*. Always keep a stash of inexpensive but unique and personal what-nots for when you're invited to someone's home. My favorite, more interesting and original than a bottle of wine or flowers, is to give a book ... a popular bestseller or a pretty, vintage volume. Be witty when you inscribe the inside cover. Hemingway's classic *A Moveable Feast* or *Chocolat* by Joanne Harris are no-brainers. What about a DVD of *Soul Food* or *Babette's Feast*? Arriving empty-handed makes for a party pariah. This is what my best buddy Glenn refers to as "showing up with arms swinging."

> *Even if you live in an apartment, an inviting atmosphere should await your guests before they even press the doorbell. Make sure the entranceway to your home is swept clean and perhaps adorned with planters or pots of flowers and maybe some tea lights. Use an old tin watering can, champagne bucket, or retro milk bottles as vases for bunches of fresh wildflowers. Fresh herbs mixed in will add rustic greenery as well as an aromatic hint of the delicious meal to come!*

Many would-be hosts are under the misconception that entertaining has to be expensive. *Au contraire.* A kitchen stocked with the staples previously mentioned may only require the main dish (for example, meat, fish, or pasta) to complete the menu. (Oftentimes, feeding four or more can be less costly than just cooking for two.) Good-tasting food, healthfully and attentively prepared, is everything a welcome guest should expect. That, and the company of fun folks. Those are the *real* ingredients for success. And that's not only free of charge, baby, it's priceless!

"No matter where I serve my guests, it seems they like my kitchen best!" That folksy old saying has adorned many a pot-holder, trivet tile, and framed needlepoint, but when it comes to *my* kitchen, I say, "Get thee into the living room and mingle!" When your party is under control, there's no need for extraneous bodies in the workplace, unless you really need a hand or there's a partic-ularly juicy morsel of gossip that cannot be shared in mixed com-pany ("While sitting in Neiman-Marcus' martini bar, I saw Raquel Welch come traipsing in wearing some too-tight jeans and on the arm of her latest, much-younger husband. Right there, he peeled off his shirt . . . while they were shopping! Can you spell *hir-suit*!?"). If said guest insists on being present while you're trying to keep on schedule, put 'em to work! One sure-fire trick for evacu-ation is to make them feel really needed. Be Garbo-esque and lay it on thick: "Dah-ling, will you pleeazze be an angel and go in there to keep the conversation going for me? I am just so reliant on your people skills . . . *what* would I do without you?!" Bang, they're gone and you can get back to your crab puffs.

If you're a couple, one person should be at the helm of the kitchen while the other tends to the guests. Single hosts should en-gage a close friend as "first mate." Never abandon your company. Would Bob Eubanks have left the Newlyweds? What kind of host would Jay Leno be if he spent all his time backstage? As Noel Coward once remarked about Joan Crawford's flair for entertain-ing: "She not only gives a party, she *goes* to it!" That's one good les-son we can learn from Mommie Dearest and even those intolerant Boy Scouts—be prepared. Then you, too, can relax and enjoy the evening as much as your friends.

"As a comforter, philosophy cannot compete with a good dinner."
—MASON COOLEY (1927–)

WHOM TO INVITE

You must create a guest list designed to delight and stimulate. If it's a birthday or anniversary celebration, you are obviously going to ask a certain group of friends or family to attend. But if you're out for a lively evening of mixed conversation, you'll want to invite an assortment—a potpourri, if you will—of personalities. I prefer telephone invites to formal ones sent through the mail. Telephone invites are more personal and I'm too impatient to wait for replies! I'm not yet a fan of the e-vite. It's too unpredictable to know whether or not someone has received it, or even how often the invitee checks e-mail.

My mother always advised against any activities in odd numbers. Someone always gets left out. A *ménage á trois* is great in theory, but the reality of it is generally a crashing disappointment, and the same goes for groups of five, seven, nine, etc.

When you consider whom you're mixing, coming up with a guest list becomes a fun strategy session. Use your common sense. Asking only gym buddies will result in Dining with Dumbbells. If it's only people associated with your job coming over, expect an evening of relentless shop-talk. Don't invite known outspoken politicos with opposing views. If one friend is a recovering alcoholic, don't invite them to break bread with hard partiers. If it's all couples, a single buddy might feel out of place or lonely. Dinner parties shouldn't be for matchmaking, unless it happens by serendipity. Then, by all means, take some credit for your (inadvertent) coupling powers.

"Mixed dinner parties of ladies and gentlemen . . . are very rare, which is a great defect in the society, not only depriving them of the most social and hospitable manner of meeting, but as leading to frequent dinner parties of gentlemen without ladies, which certainly does not conduce to refinement." —FRANCES TROLLOPE, BRITISH AUTHOR (1780–1863)

Just as you don't want your table seated with opposites, nor do you want matched sets. Think like a casting director. After all, this is your production!

Ask yourself questions like:

- Who makes me laugh?
- Who's the best storyteller?
- Who has the most offbeat job?
- Who was the last person to invite *me* over for dinner?
- Who is the most artistic?
- Whom do I want to get to know better?
- Who knows me better than anyone else?

Once you answer those honestly, you may have just come up with the perfect roster!

My dad used to advise my older sisters about making smart dating choices. "If you only date red-headed garbage men," he cautioned, "you'll marry a red-headed garbage man." Unless your redhead is Julianne Moore, follow his guidance and try to vary from your usual suspects. That also alleviates the worry that you have duplicated a spectacular menu for a repeat guest.

Stuck for something nice to say? Try taking a tip from Aristophanes: "If a woman is smart, tell her she is beautiful; if she is beautiful, tell her she is smart."

Party animals went out with the twentieth century. Don't invite chronic drinkers unless you're prepared to dip into your homeowner's or renter's insurance. You can always find out more about the subject in this book's future sequel, "Let's Dish Up an Intervention!"

Just as you don't want a guest who over-imbibes, nor do you want to contend with someone who's oversexed. If they're physically unattractive, it's obnoxious enough. If they're gorgeous, it's worse (and downright dangerous!). During an already heated game of "Taboo," I actually watched a good-looking married actor come on to my own partner . . . right in front of me and his adorable, oblivious wife ("Ohh, G*** is so open minded. He just loves gay men!"). Take it to a chat room, fella, and off of my sofa. I've found after much experience in this area (the price one pays for loving a handsome man), that the best defense is a sense of humor. Be flattered, don't cling to your mate and, in your *most* effusive manner, get the offender out of the house at the earliest opportunity. Remember to always rise above bad behavior. You'll not only have better karma, you'll ultimately be the envy of everyone and the apple of your partner's eye. (Besides, this is one cook who knows that revenge is a dish best served cold.) If the sexual attentions are thrust on you, feign ignorance, take the compliment, and cross him or her off future guest lists. True, these performances might require some molar gnashing, but kill them with kindness and reward yourself with another imaginary Best Actor Oscar for your mantel!

Don't let any friends make you feel guilty for not being asked to your latest dinner party. They should understand that you can't possibly have everybody over every time (and frankly, who'd *want* to!?). Promise to include them at a future date and if that doesn't placate them, maybe you should think about removing them from your address book, anyway.

> *"Take criticism seriously, but not personally."*
> —HILLARY RODHAM CLINTON

Another opportunity to win one of those acting prizes is when a guest offers unsolicited advice or criticism. Don't be defensive. Instead, you can lay on the charm. Thick. Let it ooze while you ask how he or she would improve the issue in question. Anyone else in earshot will be hip to your ploy (and probably amused and impressed) and Jiminy Critic will be thrilled, flattered, and likely mollified . . . until next time. Of course, you know how to avoid *that*. Adios, muchacho.

Who would be the guests at your fantasy dinner party? If you could choose any ten people, living or dead, fictitious or real, who would they be? This in itself is a party game! A very unscientific website poll revealed these as the top ten picks. Which ones would you want seated at your table?

1. *Jesus Christ*
2. *Albert Einstein*
3. *William Shakespeare*
4. *Wolfgang Amadeus Mozart*
5. *Madonna (I assume they mean the singer, not guest #1's mom)*
6. *Abraham Lincoln*
7. *John Lennon (give peas a chance)*
8. *John F. Kennedy*
9. *Marilyn Monroe (don't seat her next to guest #8)*
10. *Adolf Hitler (who let him in here!?)*

Don't be a snob. And that applies to both the host *and* guests. On a European trip, I once found myself invited to a weekend holiday at Princess Margaret's Gloucestershire country estate, with an eclectic guest list of artists, doctors, and assorted idle rich aristocrats. It turned into one of the most debauched and unfortunate excursions I've ever experienced (which is considerable if you realize that I spent my twenties in New York City during the eighties!). It would have made Heidi Fleiss blush! That was followed, coincidentally, by a week in the company of some hard-working flight attendants ("trolley dollies"), bellhops, and bartenders, whose generosity, camaraderie, and good humor proved that money certainly doesn't buy happiness. Well . . . unless you really know where to shop.

At one time or another, we've all run into snags, delays, and accidents. Realizing that most people are not innately punctual, I allow the cocktail and hors d'oeuvres hour to be the equivalent of Red Carpet Arrivals. (You know how those Hollywood types love to make an entrance!) Any guest worthy of an invitation will have arrived in plenty of time to settle in before the meal is served. You're on a schedule, after all, not running a McDonald's drive through. However, a *no-show* guest is the ultimate *no-no*, especially in this era of cellular communication. (Once arrived at a dinner party, a guest should *absolutely* turn off the cell phone. Set it to vibrate if you must, but even one ring is rude and disrespectful to everyone else.) With a good enough excuse, a no-show may have a singular reprieve, if you think his/her presence next time is worth the risk. If there is a repeat offense, it's *no-show of class* and (no matter how badly you're dying to have Mr. Brando at your table) you must not be tempted to extend any further invitation other than to an open house. Don't confuse being a gracious host with being a pushover. They're supposed to be guests, not customers.

> *"Tell the truth, work hard, and come to dinner on time."*
> —GERALD R. FORD (1913–)

Eight is generally a perfect number for a manageable dinner party, but if there is a last-minute addition ("But my brother-in-law just came into town!"), be flexible. Adopt a "the more the merrier" approach and squeeze in an extra chair. You'll be a hero and, who knows, you might also be pleasantly surprised. By the way, if you follow my guidelines, you're going to have plenty of food, anyway. Unless otherwise noted, these recipes are designed to serve that magic number of guests, eight. On the very subject of flexibility, I once acquiesced to a husband and wife inviting along their friend as my "blind date." While it might not surprise you that he came nowhere close to matching their glowing physical description, it was a stunning display of *gauche* when he appeared on my doorstep with a female tagalong! My panic disguised behind my tightest, frozen Ann Miller smile, I remembered my own advice and feigned delight. He was a complete washout, but *she* ended up being the life of the party. No wonder he brings her with him on dates!

> *"I've always said that eight was the perfect number," said Elliott, determined to look on the bright side of things. "It's intimate enough to permit of general conversation and yet large enough to give the impression of a party."* —W. SOMERSET MAUGHAM, *The Razor's Edge*

> *"The best number at a dinner party is two—myself and a damn good head waiter."* —NUBAR GULBENKIAN, BRITISH OIL TYCOON (1896–1972)

When it's time to be seated at the table, don't let everyone choose their own places. The hosts should be at opposite ends (the designated chef closest to the kitchen) to keep things lively. Split couples apart and put newer acquaintances beside older ones, with the most talkative in the middle. When it's inconsequential, I make up contests or games of chance to determine seating arrangement. For example, to welcome my friend Gena back to Los Angeles after her stint on the East Coast, I devised a personalized trivia competition to mix up the seating arrangement. Even her closest pals learned some little-known facts about her. ("To what Elvis Presley song did Gena celebrate her fortieth birthday? *Hunk-a-Hunk of Burnin' Love* is correct!") It stimulated conversation and

flattered her with the honorific attention to detail. For a fun surprise, each seat cushion was covering a prize for whoever was
seated there. These ranged from the sublime (An old *Archie* comic
book or autographed picture of Efrem Zimbalist, Jr.), to the ridiculous (a plastic egg full of "Silly Putty" or an autographed picture of
Stephanie Zimbalist). If you're clever enough to deduce on which
day of the week each guest was born, you could have a themed setting: "Monday's child is fair of face, Tuesday's child is full of grace,"
and so on. Another novel idea is to surf the Internet or Google
search engine for web pages that happen to have the names of your
friends and print them out to place at their seats. I always have fun
coming up with these for my pal Tasha Bush!

> *"Only in L.A. does one go to a dinner party where they've never met
> the host, they don't know the other guests, they're wearing a dress
> borrowed from a designer, and they get a gift bag when they leave.
> And, oh yeah, it was photographed for next month's* In Style.
> —LORI HEURING, ACTRESS, *Mulholland Drive, Runaway Jury*

Keep in mind the different possibilities created by your seating
arrangements. Write the names of your guests on scraps of paper and
experiment with the various scenarios. You might be surprised at
what you discover or may want to avoid. Maybe left-handed Louise
shouldn't be sitting to the right of gesticulating Gerry. Do you really
want to seat Big Bettina in that rickety folding chair? (I had Kathy
Najimy sit on an antique settee one time before she lost all her
weight . . . I absolutely held my breath until she arose and departed!)
    Have the table decorated appropriately and your guests will
"ooh" when you usher them into the dining room. Sometimes you
may not have enough table space available for anything too fancy,
but have some fun with motif. If it's a lighthearted group, why not
have an assortment of place mats or even dishware? Thanks to my
obsession with online auction sites like eBay and amazon.com,
I've collected an amusing array of nostalgic pieces, from the mighty
Isis to the Partridge Family. Brightly colored bowls filled with

condiments make burrito-building even more festive. Save swizzle sticks when you travel . . . these free souvenirs are fun mementoes you'll want to reuse when bartending at home. Dim the lights and flood the table with light from a hodgepodge of different candles. I've even been known to hollow out artichokes and bunches of asparagus as holders for votives and candlesticks. With all due respect, I'm *not* Martha Stewart and neither are you, so just come up with settings that look lovely to you. Get as creative as you can.

If you're going for foods that carry high risk for messiness (chili, fried chicken, etc.), the best defense is a good offense. Use big, cloth napkins that can be tossed out or washed and recycled as cleaning rags. Note: Avoid scattering around that God-awful confetti or glitter. It's toxic to animals and gets into *everything*. If you thought spinach caught between your teeth looks bad, well . . . you get the idea.

"I'll do my best and leave the rest to whatever power manages that which we cannot."
—MISS ANNIE SULLIVAN,
HELEN KELLER'S TEACHER

Remember: sh** happens. If you follow my advice and have plenty of food on hand, you will be prepared to improvise in the event of any minor mishap. I don't think there was a single night in my childhood when my mother didn't rocket up from the dinner table shrieking, "Jesus Christ! The rolls!" She'd look so dejected bringing out the blackened bricks that were once fluffy dinner rolls. Sooner or later, you'll foul something up, so having a Plan B never hurts. If your vegetables flop, pile on extra rice. If the potatoes burn, lose the salad plates and make that Caesar a side dish. If the main course is trashed, well, 'fess up and laugh it off over a gourmet pizza. Of course, it's Murphy's Law that things will go wrong when you're preparing the most expensive cut of veal you've ever purchased or while hosting the guests you most want to impress. All the more reason to handle flops with aplomb! Life's full of those little ironies—in our twenties, we trade in pimples for wrinkles . . . our thirties see health insurance go up, but car insurance go down . . . and in our forties we trade in sperm count for Propecia's hair growth.

It is bad manners to gesture with your utensils. Who are you, Norman Bates?

Realize that to be a good host, you often have to be a good sport. If you vehemently disagree with someone's opinion about something, you can't get in trouble with your mouth shut. And dishing the dirt is a diva's dinnertime delight, but exercise caution and resist saying anything at someone else's expense. If someone breaks a glass, knocks over a vase, or grabs your best bottle of vintage wine to make a *spritzer*, you must turn the other cheek. If anything's too valuable to lose, you should have locked it up beforehand.

A message of vital importance to all convened, especially couples, whether hosts or guests. If you get into a disagreement during a dinner party, nip it in the bud and immediately change the subject. It's hard to hit a moving target, so a backup or escape topic is always a smart idea. Be sure you know what movie is currently number one at the box office and the current status of J-Lo's love life! And curb your drinking. Everyone's evening will be ruined if you become quarrelsome.

Refrain from profanity. As Glenn's niece, Christine, wisely observed before she was even aged three, "*Fuck* and *Shut Up* are bad words." Whatever the problem, it will keep until later, or you'll find it was never worth the drama from the get-go. "Who's Afraid of Virginia Woolf" is only entertaining if you're watching it on video—NOT living it.

> "*At a dinner party, one should eat wisely but not too well, and talk well but not too wisely.*"   —W. SOMERSET MAUGHAM
> (1874–1966)

APPETIZERS AND BREADS

The word *appetizers* says it all. This is your chance to whet the appetites of your guests for the wonderful meal that will soon be laid before them. Some thought should be given to what you will serve as your main course so that these hors d'oeuvres can be a prelude to that style of cooking. Even the most rigid of health food fanatics can weaken for my Devilish Deviled Eggs, which are fun to eat before a meatloaf, but completely inappropriate prior to Paella!

It's nice to offer two or three different appetizers. Not everyone may want the caviar. Since you should be aware of any dietary restrictions or food allergies ahead of time, you can offer options to someone who is, say, lactose intolerant. *Austin Powers'* "Frau Farbissina," actress Mindy Sterling, is one of those delicate dieters who told me, "I have to find out what they are having ahead of time or eat before I go. Otherwise, I just stock up on bread and cheese."

You don't, however, want to go overboard and present too many choices. Limit the amount of appetizers and how long you serve. Just as you wouldn't let the cocktail hour drag on until everyone's stinko, you don't want people to belly up to the dining room table already full.

You have to give parties if you ever expect to be invited to any!

A story on food preparation: During his medical career, my father treated two elderly twin sisters. He wondered why one sister was obese, while the other maintained a healthy weight. They ate the same amount at meals and exercised equally. Dad discovered that the chubby one was the cook of the family and did all the "tasting" while making their meals. A calorie saved is a calorie earned. I think of those ladies every time I cook and am ever conscientious of how much sampling I do.

Overheard at a dinner party: "The new L.A. buzz phrase about age—owing, I assume, to our culture's improved health, nutrition, and a few generous CCs of botox injections, 'Forty is the new thirty!' "

Compliment a friend by asking him to try a taste—it's helpful to engage an objective palate. While I love spicy, my ex was known to spice up dishes to an inferno that would make Irwin Allen run for cover. You can always take the temperatures down a notch or two by mixing in honey when Honey's back is turned.

> *"A man seldom thinks with more earnestness of anything than he does of his own dinner."*   —SAMUEL JOHNSON (1709–1784)

Along with some of my favorite nibbly things to get people stoked for the main course are a few simple bread recipes you'll enjoy trying.

Chef Bruno's Salmon Mousse on White Toast

Bruno Lopez, the executive chef of Raffles, the ultra-posh restaurant in L'ermitage Beverly Hills, gave me this recipe—ideal for afternoon tea or as an appetizer to your smashing main course. Serve on your most stylish serving trays . . . it's five star!

> *Did you know that Beverly Hills is the official sister city to Cannes, France?*

2 ounces smoked salmon scraps or pieces
2 ounces cream cheese
Dash of brandy or sherry vinegar
Slices of white bread, crusts removed
4 ounces smoked salmon slices, sliced very thin
½ ounce liquid aspic (or follow package instructions to make using a
    powdered aspic)
1 ounce black caviar

In food processor, blend salmon scraps and cream cheese well, forming a mousse. Add a dash of brandy or sherry vinegar to thin it a bit.

Toast canapé bread and spread with mousse. Put one layer of very thin smoked salmon slice on bread and spray or brush on aspic. Refrigerate to set aspic. Cut into four even rectangles per slice. Dot with mousse approximately three-fourths of the way from the top point. *Gently* pipe black caviar along the base of each piece. This works well if you have the toast lined up closely and evenly. Just run the caviar along the bottom.

Easy elegance!

Aspic literally means asp, as in snake. Aspic is thought to have derived its name because the colors in the jelly resembled those of the snake. My surname, however, is derived from the Aspen tree!

Devilish Deviled Eggs

One of my guilty pleasures. Why wait for a picnic? These are great with casual meals on the patio or for afternoon get-togethers. My version is considerably healthier compared to the old-fashioned way and they look fantastic on my antique rooster deviled-eggs plate, which I stole from my mother.

Dozen eggs
5 tablespoons regular or fat-free mayonnaise
1 tablespoon pickled relish
1 teaspoon yellow mustard
1 teaspoon garlic salt
¼ teaspoon pepper
1 teaspoon minced onion
Paprika
Fresh parsley for garnish
6 green olives, sliced

Boil eggs gently for 10 minutes, run under cold water at least 30 seconds, and then shell. Cut them in half lengthwise, remove the yolks, and save them in a large mixing bowl.

Mash the yolks with a fork, adding the mayonnaise, relish, and mustard as you go. When combined, stir in the garlic salt, pepper, and onion.

Fill your sliced eggs with the yolk mixture and don't be stingy. Lightly sprinkle with paprika and garnish with the parsley and olives before putting on serving plate. *Yum!*

According to a published report, American Airlines saved $40,000 in 1987 by eliminating one olive from each salad served in first class. Talk about portion control!

Tortino di Risotto al Funghi

Since I love to entertain, it's unusual for me to throw parties at a restaurant, but when I do it's often at Pane e Vino. Their lovely, inviting ambience and consistently delicious food have made for many joyful wrap parties, New Year's Eves, and birthday celebrations. Even while spending three months teaching aerobics in a Tuscan health spa, I *never* experienced food as good as theirs! One of the owners, Rod Dyer, always welcomes me with a glass of Aperol, a mouth-watering Italian *appertivo* that you must try.

> *I can still teach an aerobics class in Italian, if called upon.* "Tonificare a la piscina! Vigoroso! Molto bene!" *"Toning by the poolside! Faster! Very good!"*

Chef Thomas Space gave me his secret recipe for this dish, my all-time favorite appetizer. It works better this way than as a main course (and also *instead* of a main course) because it is so rich. He cautions that the art of successfully making risotto is "more about touch and feeling than following scripted recipes." Experiment and master it—you and your guests will be eternally grateful! He also notes that when properly cooked, risotto should be *al dente* and requires less stock than this recipe calls for, but here the intent is to overcook so it will be sticky in texture.

¼ cup dried Porcini mushrooms
1 cup warm water (to soak mushrooms)
1 cup dry white wine
3 cups hot chicken or vegetable stock
4 tablespoons olive oil
¼ cup shallots or onion, diced
1 tablespoon chopped garlic
2 cups arborio rice
½ cup grated Parmesan cheese
1 tablespoon fresh Italian parsley, chopped
4 tablespoons butter
1 tablespoon sea salt
1 tablespoon fresh ground pepper
2 whole eggs
2 cups seasoned bread crumbs

Soak porcini in 1 cup warm water until soft, about 10 to 15 minutes. Remove mushrooms from liquid, rinse, and chop fine. Strain and reserve liquid. Combine wine, stock, and Porcini liquid in saucepan and bring to a boil. Remove from heat.

In a saucepan over medium heat, sauté onions in 2 tablespoons olive oil until translucent, about five minutes. Add garlic, rice, and mushrooms. Saute and stir until rice is well coated, about 3 to 4 minutes. Add a third of the hot stock and stir until most of the liquid has been absorbed by the rice. Repeat twice more until most of the stock has been absorbed. It is important to keep the rice moving to ensure even cooking.

Stir in Parmesan, parsley, 2 tablespoons butter, salt, and pepper. Adjust seasoning to taste. When all the moisture has been absorbed, turn risotto into a shallow pan and cool.

Form into two-inch-thick patties, any size you like. Beat eggs with a little cold water and coat the patties, then coat with seasoned bread crumbs.

To finish this amazing dish, in a skillet heat another 2 tablespoons olive oil with 2 tablespoons butter and sauté patties until crispy. Set aside in a warm oven.

For your sautéed mushroom garnish:

2 tablespoons olive oil
4 tablespoons butter
4 cloves garlic, slivered
2 pounds assorted mushrooms, sliced
½ cup white wine
2 tablespoons Italian parsley, chopped
Sea salt to taste
Fresh ground black pepper to taste
1 tablespoon white truffle oil to drizzle (worth the hunt at your specialty stores!)

Heat oil and half the butter in a skillet. Add garlic and lightly brown, about 30 to 60 seconds. Add the mushrooms and sauté until softened. Add the wine and simmer over medium heat, allowing to reduce by half. Add remaining butter and simmer until slightly thickened.

Place your warm risotto patties on a serving plate and top with the sautéed mushrooms. Finish with a sprinkle of chopped parsley, salt, pepper, and a drizzle of truffle oil. Grated Parmesan and/or baby greens make a wonderful garnish.

Serve family style and watch the delighted impression this will make on your guests! *Buon appetito!*

Holy Moley! Guacamole!

I get so excited at finding large, ripe avocados at the farmer's market that I will whip up a batch of guacamole for a quick snack anytime. This is a ridiculously simple way to make a healthy appetizer that is scooped up immediately. Delicious with baked blue corn tortilla chips. (If you're not up to making those from scratch, use a good store brand, but warm them up in the oven first.)

4 large ripe avocados
1 large lemon
1 small lime
½ cup spicy or medium salsa
¼ cup fresh cilantro, chopped
Garlic salt to taste
Ground pepper to taste
2 pounds medium-sized shrimp, washed, deveined, and cooked (optional)

Hand mash those beauteous babies and add in the juice of the whole lemon and lime.

Did you know that you will get more juice out of your citrus fruits if you microwave them for a minute?

Mix in salsa and fresh cilantro; salt and pepper to taste. If you want this to be more of a *seviche*, cut the cooked shrimp into chunks once they've cooled, and add them in.

Serve this mouth-watering concoction at room temperature, well mixed but still chunky, then watch it go, go, go! *Andale!* It is garden fresh and much tastier than store-bought that's whipped up with sour cream or mayonnaise—which, by the way, is not authentic Mexican.

East Hampton Shrimp Brochettes

I love to spend summer holidays with my friend Glenn and his partner, Dan, in their big, magnificent East Hampton home (they sold off their previous one, diminutive by comparison, to also-diminutive George Stephanopoulos and his funny wife, Alexandra Wentworth), literally just down the road from Martha Stewart's compound. They introduced me to a local personal chef, Joe Ouellette, who gave me this great cocktail party recipe for 50 brochettes (serves up to 10 guests). It's swanky, savory, and summery . . . just like a breezy Saturday night in the Hamptons with friends!

1 pound medium shrimp, shells removed, rinsed, deveined, and cut
    into halves
6 bay leaves
2 sprigs rosemary
8 cloves garlic, peeled and crushed
1 tablespoon dashi (granulated)
1 34-ounce bottle olive oil
1 cucumber, seeds removed
Sea salt and fresh ground pepper
6 sprigs mint, kept in very cold water
2 melons, made into 25 small balls with a melon baller
Extra olive oil for drizzling
25 toothpicks or mini-skewers (Joe likes to use Japanese bamboo)

Put the shrimp, bay leaves, rosemary, and garlic in a medium-sized bowl. Sprinkle the dashi over the shrimp and stir together well.

Heat the oven to 140 degrees (yes, 140 is sufficient to kill the bacteria) with the rack in the highest position.

Pour the olive oil into your largest, high-sided sauté pan, then place it over low heat. Add the seasoned shrimp to the oil. Stir to separate. Joe suggests using an instant digital thermometer to monitor the heat of the oil so that when it reaches 140 degrees (up to 15 minutes), simply give the shrimp a stir, then put it into the oven where it should remain for another quarter hour. Then, give the shrimp one more stir and shut off the oven, leaving the pan in there until you're ready to assemble the brochettes.

Slice the cucumber into chunks as thick as the small melon balls, then stir them with a sprinkle of salt in a small bowl.

Place a double layer of paper towels to cover a sheet tray and spread the cucumbers out flat in one layer, so the slices do not touch. Press another layer of paper towels atop these and repeat as necessary to use all the cucumber slices.

Pick the mint leaves off the sprigs and lay them onto a paper towel.

To assemble the brochettes, line up your ingredients in the following order:

- Toothpicks
- Cucumbers
- Pan of shrimp
- Mint leaves
- Melon
- Sheet tray

Place a plate in front of the pan to catch the oil dripping from the shrimp as you assemble.

Use a toothpick to skewer a cucumber (not too far up the toothpick), then a shrimp. Fold a mint leaf into fours and skewer it next to the shrimp. Put a melon ball just to the end of the toothpick and place it on the sheet tray, keeping the part of the toothpick that will be picked up very clean.

Just before you transfer the brochettes onto a serving platter, sprinkle them with salt and pepper, then drizzle on a little fresh olive oil.

Fab Frittata au Gratin

A little more unusual than a quiche, this fun and easy dish can be cooked, cut into slices, and eaten right from the skillet. I think that's best for brunch, however, so when serving as a hot appetizer, I recommend squares that are brownie sized.

1 medium all-purpose potato
½ cup asparagus tips
2 tablespoons olive oil
Sprig of fresh rosemary, chopped
Salt and pepper, to taste
4 eggs
2 tablespoons Parmesan cheese
½ cup shredded Cheddar cheese
Chopped parsley

Peel potato, boil 15 to 20 minutes, then slice. Meanwhile, wash the asparagus, snap off thick ends, and blanch the tips in five cups of simmering water for 2 to 3 minutes. Drain.

Saute the potato slices and rosemary in one tablespoon of oil until the potato begins to crisp, about 10 minutes. Shake a little salt and pepper in with the asparagus tips, add them to the potatoes, and continue to sauté for another 2 to 3 minutes. Remove from heat.

Preheat the broiler. On the stovetop, heat a nonstick skillet with a tablespoon of oil. Beat the eggs with a pinch of salt and pepper and pour into skillet over low heat. When the eggs just begin to set, add the vegetable mixture on top of the eggs. Sprinkle on the Parmesan and Cheddar cheeses.

Immediately place the skillet under the broiler (for Heaven's sake, wear an oven mitt). It will take less than 3 minutes for the frittata to begin to sizzle. Remove from heat, sprinkle with parsley, and let cool.

Great gift idea! My late mentor and friend, the venerable Mary Stuart—best known as the long suffering, oft-married, "Joanne Gardner Barron Tate Reynolds Vincente Tourneur" on Search for Tomorrow—once presented me with a cast iron omelet pan, saying that every bachelor should know how to make an omelet. She was, as always, absolutely right! Even leftover Chinese food tastes good in an omelet. Mary taught me that the trick was to fold and remove the eggs from the pan and allow it a minute to finish cooking right on the plate. I still have that pan and think of Mary every time I use it. The gift of crockery and kitchenware make surprisingly personal and treasured memories. Hail Mary!

Olivia DeHave-to-Have-a-Tapenade

The French have an idiom, *serviable*. I asked *mon ami*, Georges, owner of my favorite Los Angeles bistro, *Brasserie des Artistes*, to try to translate it into English for me and he provided a most excellent definition: "To be *serviable*, you help others in a very gentle way. You use your natural manners to try and help everybody." I thought that was a *tres* lovely explanation of a quality every host/hostess should aspire to achieve. So in the spirit of such good taste, here is a French recipe for a savory appetizer that will surely be devoured *toute suite*!

½ pound Mediterranean black olives (pitted, if possible)
6 small anchovy fillets
1 heaping tablespoon capers
½ teaspoon fresh thyme
1 teaspoon lemon juice
2 tablespoons olive oil

If your olives aren't already pitted, use a mortar and pestle to gently press out the pits. Add the next 3 ingredients and lemon juice into the mortar, mashing them until a paste begins to form. Continue grinding, gradually adding in the oil.

Keep your tapenade covered in the refrigerator until ready to serve on toast points, crackers, or crusty baguette slices.

If you're the type who likes to give gifts of homemade jarred foods, this is *formidable*!

Stuffed-Up Mushrooms

You can tell you've really grown up when these are the kind of mushrooms you serve at a party. These are sure fire, low fat, and quick to fix.

3 dozen large mushrooms, brushed clean
3 tablespoons garlic, minced
1 tablespoon butter
8 ounces bulk sausage (I like spicy chorizo)
½ cup grated Parmesan
½ cup seasoned bread crumbs
¼ cup fresh parsley or cilantro, chopped
Red pepper flakes to taste

Preheat your oven to 400 degrees. Remove the stems from the mushrooms, chop and sauté them with the butter and garlic for 2 to 3 minutes. Brown the sausage with this mixture, 8 to 10 minutes, and stir in the remaining ingredients. When well-mixed, remove from heat and stuff your mushroom caps, then bake them in the oven on a non-stick cookie sheet for 5 to 7 minutes.

Papa's Lobster B.L.T.

Spago's lunch menu includes their spectacular version of a Lobster B.L.T., so I came up with a recipe that lets you revel in its deliciousness in a bite-sized canapé version. Lobster always reminds me of my own old man of the sea, my dad. He's an Ernest Hemingway lookalike and tells the story of how, during the Korean War, he came to crave the crustacean courtesy of the literary legend himself.

While serving as a navy doctor aboard the *U.S.S. Sphinx*, "The skipper announced that we would spend the weekend in Havana, but no overnight leave. My friend was a lieutenant senior grade engineering officer and we went ashore midday, equipped with cameras. We stopped at the famous *Floradita* bar for lunch and a beer. An older man sat at a rear table with a bottle of rum and invited us to join him. Uniforms do help! He offered us lunch and mine was lobster. It was delicious but I did not admit then that it was the first time I had ever tasted it! By this time, I had recognized him to be the famous author, Ernest Hemingway."

I told the gorgeous Mariel this story the night I met her; she loved it and observed that she could see the resemblance in me, as well. Sweet!

Here's a recipe *both* Papas would enjoy!

1 cup regular or fat-free mayonnaise
3 tablespoons fresh lemon juice
1 tablespoon minced onion
1 tablespoon sweet pickle relish
2 teaspoons sea salt
½ teaspoon Tabasco
½ teaspoon cayenne pepper
2 Roma tomatoes, chopped
½ pound crispy bacon, crumbled into bits
1 pound fresh, cooked lobster, chopped
Toasted baguette slices, toast points, or hearty crackers
Butter lettuce leaves
Parsley for garnish

In a medium bowl, prepare your tartar sauce by mixing together mayonnaise, lemon juice, onion, relish, and salt. Add Tabasco and cayenne for a little kick and a little color. Add chopped tomatoes and bacon bits. Finally, fold in the chopped lobster meat and refrigerate until ready to serve.

Top toast slices or crackers with small lettuce leaves and dollops of the chilled, chunky salad. Garnish with tiny bits of parsley.

"As I ate the oysters with their strong taste of the sea and their faint metallic taste that the cold white wine washed away, leaving only the sea taste and the succulent texture, and as I drank their cold liquid from each shell and washed it down with the crisp taste of the wine, I lost the empty feeling and began to be happy and to make plans." —ERNEST HEMINGWAY, *A Moveable Feast*

A Star Is Born Caviar

So showy, it's almost *too* much. But, Esther Blodgett/Vicki Lester, that's why we love it!

10 large red beets
3 large jicama
Star-shaped cookie cutter
1½ cups regular or fat-free sour cream
1 small jar of caviar
Sprigs of fresh fennel

Boil the beets, about 45 to 60 minutes, allow to cool, and peel. Wash and peel the jicama, including the fibrous layer under the skin. Cut both vegetables into one-quarter-inch round slices. Use a cookie cutter to cut the centers of the slices into stars. Valentine's Day? Switch to a heart-shaped cookie cutter. You get the idea.

Spoon or use a pastry bag to position the sour cream in small dots atop each beet. Stir beet juice into the remaining sour cream to color, then dot the jicama stars, too.

Top with a little arrangement of caviar, garnishing with fennel. Ta da!

Nuts About Paté

Double dippers, beware. This is so de-lish that no cracker, carrot stick, or toast point is immune to its siren call. It's also a great alternative for your sensitive vegetarian friends who'd rather pickle their own livers than eat that of a duck. An added bonus is that it's as simple to prepare as it is great to eat. This will appetize eight.

   2 slices whole wheat bread, crusts removed
   ¾ cup low-fat milk
   2 cups assorted nuts, chopped (I like to mix
      pecans, cashews, and walnuts)
   1½ cups Romano or Parmesan cheese, shredded
   2 garlic cloves, chopped
   3 tablespoons olive oil
   Salt and pepper to taste
   Radicchio for garnish

Soak the bread slices in the milk, then mash with the nut mixture, cheese, garlic, and oil. Season generously with salt and pepper, then chill in a small serving bowl. When ready to serve, plop it out of the bowl upside down onto an elegant serving dish. Garnish with radicchio shavings. If radicchio is too strong a flavor for your palate, try chives or old reliable parsley.

Then, *poof!* Watch it disappear!

Louan's Cheesy Spinach Balls

I first met glam Louan Gideon on the set of *One Life to Live* and we connected instantly, going on to work together again on the now defunct *Search for Tomorrow*. We're both in Los Angeles now and she's one of my most beautiful friends, inside and out. She's also funny as hell. I will never forget soaking in the pool of the Beverly Hills Four Seasons Hotel and her asking the cabana boy to take back the "unpopped grannies" from her bowl of popcorn to be re-popped. Who says we Angelenos are spoiled?

To see this long, tall, Texan gal, you'd never guess she can cook, too (in addition to being a licensed Feng Shui practitioner, magnet therapist, piano tuner, real estate agent, and singer, just to name a few of her sidelines). Here's one of her favorite party dishes. Save for a big bash because this makes 96(!) balls, which you will keep in the freezer, uncooked, until needed.

    2 10-ounce packages frozen chopped spinach
    1 large onion, chopped
    ¾ cup butter
    1 8-ounce package cornbread stuffing mix
    5 eggs
    ½ cup Parmesan, grated
    1 tablespoon garlic powder
    1 tablespoon pepper
    1 teaspoon salt
    1 teaspoon thyme

Cook the spinach per the package instructions, drain, and set aside. Sauté the onion with butter until transparent.

Add stuffing mix and onion to spinach. Beat eggs well, then add to mixture. Add Parmesan cheese, then garlic powder. Next, use your hands to thoroughly mix in the pepper, salt, and thyme. Chill the mixture for one hour.

Roll the mixture into walnut-sized balls and place in tightly closed plastic bags. Freeze them until your party.

Bake the spinach balls on a non-stick cookie sheet at 400 degrees for 20 minutes. Serve hot.

Chic Chicon au Four (Baked Belgian Endives)

You probably guessed by now that I love the tabloids. I don't just thumb through them at the checkout line, I proudly purchase them! *National Enquirer* columnist Jose Lambiet not only cooks on a deadline, but in the kitchen as well. Hailing from picturesque Aubel, Belgium, he shares with us one of his old family recipes: the epitome of Belgian farm cooking. To calculate serving amounts, plan on 2 to 3 endives per person.

8 endives (adjust as needed)
2 tablespoons butter, softened
2 to 3 tablespoons flour
2 cups whole milk
8 ounces imported Swiss cheese, such as Gruyere, grated
Salt and pepper to taste
1 teaspoon nutmeg
8 thin slices of a salty ham, one for each endive

Remove outer leaves from the endives to remove any hard bottoms (ouch!). Remove hearts and discard (sounds like something my ex would do). Place whole endives in a steam rack in a pot with a small amount of water. Steam for 15 to 20 minutes or until the endives turn a gray, translucent color. They should be soft, so that a fork goes easily through the thick end.

Preheat oven to 375 degrees. While the endives steam, prepare the cheese sauce. Blend butter and flour in a pot over medium heat until it has a paste-like consistency. Whisk in milk slowly. Cook on the stove, whisking until milk/butter mixture boils into a smooth sauce. Reduce heat immediately and begin adding about half of the grated cheese, a pinch at a time until fully melted. Reserve half the cheese for topping. Add salt, pepper, and finally the nutmeg.

Remove the endives from the steamer and wrap each one with a slice of salty ham and place them flat, side by side, in a square, oven-proof dish. Pour the cheese sauce over them until all the endives are covered. Sprinkle the remaining Swiss cheese over the top.

Bake uncovered until the cheese is brown and bubbly, about 10 minutes.

This fab, fattening fare should be served with dipping bread or mashed potatoes. Pour plenty of Bordeaux and gossip about those clever Belgians. They know so much more about cuisine than just chocolates and waffles!

Fried Artichokes (*Like Nonna Used to Make!*)

Sometimes you dread when the person sitting next to you on the airplane starts up a conversation. Other times, you make a friend for life, like I did when Brooklyn bombshell Norma Vally chatted me up on a flight from New York City. Turned out we have the same talent agent (Norma's the host of the TV show *Toolbelt Diva*) as well as the same passion for fried artichokes. Proving she's one of those self-professed "chicks who fix," she emailed me this stupendous way to prepare them, which was handed down to her by her mom and Nonna (Grandma). Fried sides like this, Norma says, are called *contorni*—which translates to "going around" the main dish. You'll be delighted to have them going around yours, to be sure!

6 baby artichokes
Juice of ½ lemon
1 cup flour
2 eggs
½ cup Romano cheese, grated
¼ cup fresh parsley, chopped
1 tablespoon fresh mint, chopped (optional)
1 cup olive oil
2 cloves garlic
Salt and pepper

Cut the tops off the artichokes (Norma: "so they look like they just got buzz cuts!"). Pull off stray leaves from the outside. Cut off the dark parts of the stem (Norma: "the part that looks too dry to eat") and place each artichoke on its side and start cutting slices lengthwise, one-quarter-inch thick. Norma assures that there's no need to remove the choke. (Norma: "because these baby-sized babies have chokes that won't, well, choke you.")

Boil a quart of water. Remove from heat. Add artichoke slices, lemon juice, and salt. Let stand in the pot about 5 minutes with cover on. Drain artichokes and pat dry with paper towels.

Coat artichokes in flour. (Nonna used to put the flour and slices in a paper bag and shake them.)

Beat the eggs, then add the cheese and parsley.

Heat half of the olive oil in a frying pan. Throw a clove of garlic into the oil for added flavor. Individually dip artichoke slices in the egg mixture so they're fully coated, then place in heated oil. Flip them when they're golden brown and cook on the other side. Remove and drain on a plate lined with paper towels. Repeat for second batch, adding more oil.

Add salt, pepper and mint to taste. Serve warm or at room temperature with lemon wedges.

Sure beats airplane food, eh, Norma!?

Marathon Muffins

I recently completed my fifth marathon with a personal best of 4:23:35. In fact, it's a safe bet that if I'm not working or entertaining, I'm running. Obviously, I have become addicted to the training process required for long-distance running, so much so that I created my own patented fitness program, The Brains and Brawn Workout™. One of the perks of logging all those miles is the joy of being able to pig out on carbs with no guilt! Here is a recipe I perfected for delicious, quick-energy muffins for when you're on the go. They're also great served in a big basket the next time you're having a picnic or barbeque. My motto: "Bodies in motion, *stay* in motion!"

2 cups all-purpose flour
⅓ cup brown sugar
⅓ cup granulated sugar
2 teaspoons baking powder
⅛ teaspoon salt
1 banana, mashed
⅓ cup butter, melted
⅓ cup milk
2 eggs, lightly beaten
1 teaspoon vanilla
Optional: Toss in a handful
   of white chocolate chips or
   chopped nuts

In a large bowl, sift together flour, sugars, baking powder, and salt. In a separate bowl, mix the mashed banana with the melted butter, milk, eggs, and vanilla.

Make a well in the dry ingredients. Add the liquid mixture and stir just until combined. If desired, add in chocolate morsels and/or nuts.

Spray muffin tins with cooking spray, divide the batter evenly in tins, and bake at 400 degrees for 10 to 15 minutes. Depending on the size, this should yield slightly more than a dozen muffins. You can check for doneness with a toothpick. These are quick and easy, because you're on the run!

My running buddy, Jerry, has a handy tip for keeping sweat out of your eyes when you're out there pounding the pavement mile after mile: apply regular lip balm over your eyebrows. It repels the perspiration from your forehead, to keep from blurring your vision. After all, you have to keep a sharp lookout for any hotties running in your direction! Every Saturday, we spot JAG hunk David James Elliott out there shirtless and sweating for all to see. Ahhh, ya gotta love Hollywood!

Nasty Nellie's Bitchin' Scones

Growing up in the seventies with the name Nelson, you can imagine the comparisons with Nellie Olesen that were heaped upon me. But Alison Arngrim, the actress who immortalized the Little Bitch on the Prairie, is one of the nicest, funniest, and most hospitable gals in town. If you're lucky enough to be invited over, do not refuse! You'll get to see her sno-globe collection and Betty Boop memorabilia, and be served hot beverages on the Little House silver tea set she received as a gift from Michael Landon.

1¾ cups flour, sifted
2¼ teaspoons double-acting baking powder
1 tablespoon sugar
2 teaspoons salt

¼ **cup cold butter**
2 eggs
⅓ **cup cream**

Preheat oven to 450 degrees and sift dry ingredients together into a bowl.

Cut the butter into the flour mixture, Alison advises, "until it's like small peas. Use a pastry blender if you know what you're doing, or two knives if you don't." She's so bossy!

Beat eggs separately in another bowl, setting aside 2 tablespoons of beaten egg for brushing over the scones prior to baking.

Mix the cream into the beaten eggs. Make a well in the dry ingredients and pour the liquid into it. Stir just enough to get it mixed. Scones are not, Alison points out, to be beaten or whipped. She saves that torture for poor little Half Pint, I suppose.

Alison: "You might at this point add any extras like chocolate chips, blueberries, etc. These things are, of course, actually total blasphemies on the face of holy scone-dom. The only thing that really belongs in a scone are currants or sultanas [white raisins]."

Place the dough on a lightly floured surface and pat down until it's about one-quarter-inch thick. No rolling. Cut into the classic triangular or diamond shapes.

Place on non-stick cookie sheet, brush with the beaten egg previously set aside. Sprinkle with a little sugar and bake, about 15 minutes.

Serve with lots of butter, jam, jelly, marmalade, Devonshire cream, and "other gooey, disgusting things. Wash it down with big pots of Earl Grey tea and tiny little glasses of sherry."

Wouldn't Harriet Olesen be proud!?

Bread from the Ex-Files

Sometimes breaking up a long-term relationship leaves you with nothing but bitterness and heartache. I was lucky and got custody of the dog *and* this awesome, fool-proof bread recipe. Until you run out and buy that bread machine, try this one.

Mother always says, "There's no cure for an old love like a new love! And make sure the next one loves you just a little bit more than you love them!"

½ cup cornmeal
⅓ cup packed brown sugar
1 teaspoon salt
⅔ cup boiling water
⅓ cup vegetable oil
3 cups all-purpose flour
1½-2 cups whole wheat flour
1 package active dry yeast
1 8-ounce can of cream-style corn
½ 8-ounce can stewed tomatoes

Preheat oven to 375 degrees.

In a medium-sized bowl, stir together the cornmeal, sugar, and salt. Stir in the boiling water and the oil. Let mixture cool until warm, stirring occasionally.

In a large bowl, stir together 1 cup of the all-purpose flour, and the yeast. Add cornmeal mixture and the cans of corn and tomatoes. Beat with an electric mixer on low speed for 30 seconds, constantly scraping the sides of the bowl. Next, beat on high for 3 minutes, while using a spoon to stir in as much of the remaining all-purpose and whole wheat flour as you can.

Knead the dough on a lightly floured surface, working in enough of the remaining flour (both types) to make it smooth and elastic. (No more than 8 minutes.)

Shape dough into a ball, place in a lightly greased bowl. Turn once to grease surface. Cover the bowl and let dough rise in a warm place. In one to two hours, it will double in size. (Hey, sometimes it used to take *him* that long!)

Punch down the dough and knead again on the lightly floured surface. (If it helps, visualize your ex during the punching stage. *Wham!* Cheaper than therapy!) Divide the dough in half, cover, and let it rest for about 10 minutes.

While you figure out what color bread machine you will buy, grease a large baking sheet.

Shape the dough halves into separate round loaves. Place them on the baking sheet, cover, and let rise for another hour. He used to brush the bread with egg whites before baking to give it a glossy surface. Sparkle Nealy!

Bake 35 to 40 minutes.

A heavy, satisfying bread that will keep you warm on those cold, lonely nights! And when you wake up alone (but not *lonely!*), it fries up superbly as French toast!

Once the bread is on your bread plate, you never want to cut it with a knife. Simply tear off a bite-sized piece. As tempting as it might be to mop up the last of the sauce on your plate with a piece of bread, resist! Hey, and get your elbows off the table!

SOUPS, SALADS, AND SIDES

Since I so enjoy offering friends the entire "home cookin'" experience, I love to serve soup as a first course (as long as it isn't the dog days of the Santa Ana wind season). No dish can surpass the warm and comforting satisfaction of a hearty soup, and I like to get very creative with my concoctions!

If you prefer, salads are great first courses. Since it seems hypocritical to ruin the nutritious benefits of vegetables, I always opt for low-fat, healthy dressings as well. Save your caloric intake for naughtier gastronomic endeavors. You might like some of these well enough that you want to make them into side dishes to accompany your main course. Why not?

Hang on to those hot mustard packets the next time you order in Chinese food. These are delicious mixed into balsamic dressings!

When not serving a salad course, a simple green salad with oil and vinegar should be offered for guests to enjoy before, during, or after their main course. Try putting out a few dishes of slivered almonds or sesame seeds for sprinkling on top. Likewise, make warm loaves of your homemade breads available at each end of the table.

Pet peeve: Reusing eating utensils. Later in this book you will find a diagram of a standard place setting. (After all, if you're going to set the table, do it correctly!) A salad fork is for salad and not to be reused. A good host will clear it away and it won't be seen again. Help others learn this very basic act of social grace. If you are in a restaurant and a waiter dares to put your used utensil back on your place setting, politely inform him/her that you would like a new one. This essential element of breeding is as important as conversational French or a passable game of tennis. (Only kidding, but come on— reusing a salad fork for your fish course is just plain gross!)

After everyone has finished the first course, you may clear the table. Do not stack or scrape any dishes in the presence of your guests. Not a pretty sight. Hopefully, you kept the kitchen clean as you were preparing the meal (clean as you go!), so you can just load the plates directly into the dishwasher or into some soapy water.

I learned that cleanliness really *is* next to Godliness in my Dickensian prep school. They had me slopping lunch plates directly off the conveyor belt and into a large pail. I believe I was the only student in the history of Westtown Friends School who insisted on wearing disposable plastic gloves to work kitchen duty! I was eventually "promoted" to sorting silverware, scalding hot from the dishwasher. This higher education only left me with scarred fingertips! Remember that the next time the subject of school vouchers is debated!

Never assume your company won't see "behind the scenes" in the kitchen. Helpful Hannah may decide to bring in some plates, and you'll want to be proud of the environment in which you have prepared their meal.

Luscious Lentil Soup

Whenever I put on a few pounds, this is my "secret weapon" for fat-busting. I enjoy it for a day or two and that extra weight ends up all gone, along with the soup! If *you're* on a diet, go ahead and make plenty—it freezes well, too.

Soups are a great venue for bay leaves. They're easy to grow and my old place was covered with them. Fortunately, it's now rented by an actress friend of mine, and she still lets me raid her garden. As for the sausage listed below, you can substitute whatever your heart desires—beef, poultry, pork or, like my pal Tasha, even tofu.

This recipe will easily serve 8, but if it's just for the two of you, why not free up some time for your soap operas by skipping over the lentil preparation and start with 2 large cans of good canned lentil soup as your base. Just a suggestion.

1 pound dried lentils
3 quarts low-fat, low-sodium chicken stock
2 bay leaves
Garlic salt and pepper, to taste
1 teaspoon Worcestershire sauce
Tabasco, to taste
1 teaspoon celery salt
½ teaspoon caraway seeds
8 ounces vegetarian sausage
2 16-ounce bottles of dark beer
2 cups diced celery
1 cup diced carrots
1 cup diced onions
1 tablespoon cilantro, chopped

Pick over and rinse the lentils, then put them in a large pot with the chicken stock, bay leaves, garlic salt, pepper, Worcestershire, Tabasco, celery salt, and caraway. Bring to a boil, stirring occasionally.

Meanwhile, prepare your vegetarian sausage according to package instructions, pour off any excess oils, and blot with paper towels. Then add the sausage to your steaming cauldron of magically slimming soup!

Turn heat way down to a simmer. After 15 minutes, add 16 ounces of beer. In another 15, add another bottle. Smells great!

Stir in your celery, carrots, onions, and cilantro and allow to simmer until the vegetables are tender, about fifteen minutes. Serve with a loaf of hearty caraway bread.

Unbeatable Black Bean Salad

Mmm-mm-good stuff. Whether all on its own, or as a side with burritos, or on the picnic table, this salad is best served fresh and cold. And, this is so easy, it's downright ridiculous. Tasty and colorful, too . . . like you, sweetie.

    4 cups cooked black beans (I use canned beans, drained, or frozen
        when I can find them)
    1 large red bell pepper, cored, seeded, and minced within an inch of
        its life
    4 scallions, chopped fine
    ½ cup hot salsa
    ½ cup olive oil
    Juice of one large lemon
    6 tablespoons fresh chopped cilantro
    ⅓ cup yellow corn
    1 teaspoon garlic salt

Toss all of the ingredients together and refrigerate. If you're smart, you'll make extra to enjoy for tomorrow's lunch. Also great on a relish tray or to take to a pot luck.

Salade Nicoise Comme la Mere de Jose Eber

Pop culture's favorite cowboy-hatted coiffure, José Eber, is a charming Frenchman with a passion for beautiful things. When it comes to cuisine, he tells me that nothing beats his own mother's traditional Salade Nicoise . . . and since he is a native of Nice, the salad's birthplace, I believe him!

Salad ingredients:

8 small new potatoes
4 eggs
2 1-pound tuna fillets
Lettuce hearts
4 tomatoes, sliced
Small black olives
Anchovies

Boil potatoes in salted water 20 to 30 minutes until skins come off easily. Meanwhile, cook eggs 10 minutes in gently boiling water, then run under cold tap water for 30 seconds. Remove shells and slice.

Broil tuna fillets at 500 degrees, 4 minutes on each side.

Fill a large bowl with lettuce hearts, tomatoes, egg and potato slices, olives, and anchovies. Toss all ingredients, then flake tuna on top. Time to make the vinaigrette!

Vinaigrette:

2 tablespoons dijon mustard
Salt and pepper
Juice of 4 fresh lemons
4 tablespoons olive oil
1 tablespoon white wine vinegar
4 to 6 small white onions, finely chopped

Whisk ingredients thoroughly in a small bowl, then transfer into a decanter so that each guest may dress their own salad.

José recommends serving the eggs, potatoes, and tuna warm to "wake up all the flavors" of this southern French favorite!

> *"In Amsterdam or Brussels, the men have great big muscles,*
> *But they're nicer . . . much nicer . . . in Nice!"*
>   —SANDY WILSON'S *The Boyfriend*

Classic Corn Chowder

Serves 8. If there's a little extra, don't tell your guests—save it for your own snack, later. This delicious soup with a loaf of your homemade oat bread is really a meal in itself.

1 medium-sized potato
2 red onions, diced
2 tablespoons butter
2 cups clam juice
½ cup red peppers, diced
2 cans creamed corn or 2 ½ cups frozen
½ teaspoon dried thyme
Cilantro, finely chopped, to taste
Paprika, to taste
Garlic salt, to taste
2 cups whole milk
Tabasco, to taste

Peel potato and boil for about 20 minutes, until it slides easily off a fork when pricked. Dice.

In a wonderful old soup pot, brown your onion in the butter over medium heat, then add clam juice, potato, peppers, and corn. While this simmers, you may add the thyme and sprinkle in some cilantro, paprika, and garlic salt.

After five minutes, add the milk and heat until it reaches a boil. Give the soup a shot of Tabasco sauce. Reduce to low heat and cover until it's time to serve.

This colorful soup gets thicker and more delicious the longer it simmers. Sometimes I even make it the night before and reheat it an hour before serving. If an unexpected throng turns up, it's just as delicious when you stretch it out with chicken broth and some extra corn. Don't give me a hard time about not using fresh corn, which I would need to remove from the cobs and puree in a blender. What a pain! You don't need Mapquest to use a shortcut, now and then.

Do you know the real difference between green and red bell peppers? Red ones are ripe. All peppers start out green but as they sunbathe and redden, they become sweeter and more nutritious, loaded with Vitamins A and C. Maybe that's why they're also more expensive!

Aunt Joanie Raindrops' Soup for a Rainy Day

Watching Rosalind Russell, didn't you always wish you'd had an Auntie Mame? I'm fortunate enough to have my divine Aunt Joanie Raindrops, who is close to it. She earned that nickname when I was about three years old and she whisked me out into a summer rainstorm to dance, sing, and revel in Mother Nature's cooling display (granted, she's a bit of a hippie). My overprotective mother was frantic, but I didn't catch a cold and I learned that there's nothing wrong with getting wet (unless you've just sprayed your new hairdo. Of course, José Eber told me there's no such thing as a bad hair day, since these days, "Anything goes!").

Aunt Joanie Raindrops has burned her bra, worked peace missions in the Far East, practiced EST, and still sings three-part harmony with my mom and their third Musketeer, Aunt Dottie. And that's just what I *know about*! I knew she'd have a perfect rainy day recipe to contribute to this effort and she excitedly sent me this one. It's much tastier than the rattlesnake canapés Auntie Mame used to serve *her* guests! Not surprisingly, Aunt Joanie's measurements aren't precise, but she is quick to point out: "Herbs and spices are to food as colors are to a painting. Taste and play with them!

"As you know," she continued in her missive, "I love to be in a pouring, summer rain. I love to stroll without an umbrella, or just stand naked in the downpour when circumstances permit. Martinis are great to drink in the rain, always with three olives for 'I . . . Love . . . You!' After that, I like to cozy up with a glorious soup like this one."

1 whole butternut squash
Canned chicken broth, to cover squash
½ cup milk or cream
3 tablespoons chopped parsley
Croutons
Sliced almonds
Pinch nutmeg
1 tablespoon grated parmesan or your choice of cheese
Herbs and spices (rosemary, thyme, whatever's fresh and natural!)
1 medium onion, chopped

Bake the whole squash at 350 degrees until it is fork-tender (30-40 min). Peel, cut lengthwise, and scoop out the seeds. Cut into chunks and simmer in chicken broth.

Put on your tie-dyed apron and start experimenting with your spices per Aunt Joanie's instructions until the soup is aromatic. Then puree mixture in a blender or food processor before adding milk or cream to desired consistency. Return to heat until piping hot.

Sprinkle with fresh herbs, croutons, and almonds. Serve with crunchy, toasted French bread topped with melted cheese.

Make a lot so you'll have extra to take to your yoga instructor, tea leaf reader, or spiritual guide.

Sleek Leek and Potato Soup

4 tablespoons butter
8 leeks, sliced thinly and rinsed thoroughly
4 celery stalks, sliced thin
4 cups low-fat, low-sodium chicken broth
3 large potatoes, diced
Salt and pepper, to taste
3 cups low-fat milk
Chives

Melt the butter in a large pot and add the leeks and celery. Cook over medium heat, stirring often, for 10 minutes. Stir in half of the chicken broth and potatoes. Add salt and pepper. Cook until the potatoes are soft, about 10 minutes.

Pour half the soup into a blender with the milk and puree. Return the mixture to the pot and cook for 10 minutes. Whole milk makes the soup even thicker, if you prefer.

Sprinkle the individual bowls of soup with chives and coarse black pepper before serving.

To properly eat soup, fill your spoon by skimming it across the top of your serving, away from you. Never grip the side of your bowl or tip it to lap up the remaining dregs. Relax, Oliver Twist, there will be more food coming. You don't have to wipe up every drop. You know better than to leave the soup spoon in your bowl; it should come to rest on the plate that's underneath.

Cold Cuke Soup to Warm a Lonely Heart

Sometimes a cucumber is better than a boyfriend (wink wink!). This use for one certainly is: It's both a soup *and* a salad!

6 medium-sized cucumbers, peeled and seeded
2 tablespoons garlic, minced
1 small onion, chopped
4 cups low-fat, low-sodium chicken broth
1 cup low-fat or fat-free sour cream
3½ tablespoons white wine vinegar
Tabasco to taste
Salt to taste

Use your blender to puree the cucumbers one batch at a time, with the garlic, onion, and 1½ cups of the chicken broth. Pour into a large bowl and add the rest of the broth, sour cream, vinegar, and dashes of Tabasco and salt. Whisk together until smooth and completely combined.

Chill at least 4 hours, then stir well before serving. Pretty garnishes could include chopped parsley, scallions, or toasted slivered almonds.

Krispy Korean Kole-Slaw

Another slimming recipe, this one adapted from the Korean staple *kim-chi*. When I was small, our family had a Korean maid named Soon-Rye (pronounced *Soo-oon Yea*) who weaned us on this delicious side/salad. In keeping with the times, I've gotten rid of the MSG (Do they even still *make* Accent?).

¼ cup red vinegar
1 tablespoon low-sodium soy sauce
1½ teaspoons sugar
1 teaspoon dry mustard
1¼ tablespoons ginger powder
½ teaspoon cayenne pepper
1 tablespoon olive oil
4 cups cabbage, shredded
½ cup celery, diced
½ cup onion, diced
1 cup red and green peppers, diced
1 cup carrots, shredded
3 tablespoons parsley, chopped
Crispy Chinese noodles (optional)

In a small bowl, mix vinegar, soy sauce, sugar, mustard, ginger, cayenne, and oil.

In a large bowl, mix your cabbage, celery, onion, peppers, carrots, and parsley. Add the mixture from the small bowl and marinate at least an hour. Toss the slaw well and serve in small bowls, topping with a sprinkle of crispy noodles, if desired.

Kids: When's dinner, Soon-Rye?
Soon: Soon!
Kids: Yea!

Bermuda-ful Baked Onions

If you've never been to the lovely British isle of Bermuda (and no, it's not located in the Triangle!), do yourself a favor and save your pence to take the vacation of a lifetime! The shopping, the dining, the beaches, the nightlife . . . this little Atlantic hideaway has it all! Just ask part-time residents Ross Perot, Michael Douglas and Catherine Zeta-Jones, or David Bowie and Iman. While visiting, be sure to pick up some Outerbridge's Sherry Peppers for your pantry. Henry VIII Restaurant is the place to go for a steak. And a harbor-side, candlelit dinner for two (I recommend the local catch of the day and a bowl of spicy chowder) at the Waterloo House is the most romantic setting you will ever find west of Paris's Left Bank.

A word of caution, however. Homosexuality was only recently struck from Bermuda's law books as a punishable crime, and while there are as many gay people there as anywhere else (*believe me!*), demonstrative behavior is distinctly frowned upon, forcing many of the cruise ship queens and tropic tribesmen to keep their activities behind closed doors. Tourism has been way down in recent years, so perhaps they'll catch up with the times and covet the spending power of gay travelers.

A delicious recipe to complement your meal or to adapt as an appetizer is the Baked Bermuda Onion. While the onion's peak time is April through June and it may be a challenge to find it at your produce stand, you can substitute any large, meaty onion that looks good to you. There are no specific measurements for this one, you have to sort of trust your instincts. You can almost feel the gentle island breeze!

8 large Bermuda onions
Pats of butter
Salt and pepper, to taste
Rum, to taste
Honey, to taste
Brown sugar, to taste
Herbs de Provence,* to taste
Dash of nutmeg

Cut onions into quarters and place them in a buttered casserole pan. Top each quarter with pats of butter and sprinkle liberally with salt and pepper. Drizzle several tablespoons of rum, honey, and brown sugar over the top, followed by a generous amount of the herbs and a dash of nutmeg.

Bake covered at 350 degrees for 30 to 45 minutes until tender.

*Herbs de Provence is traditionally a mix of marjoram, savory (a perennial European mint), basil, rosemary, and thyme. Blending these ingredients in a pretty sachet also makes a *très charmant* keepsake for your dinner guests.

Did you know my dad, also named Nelson Aspen, literally wrote the book on the history of Bermudian currency? Oddly enough, it's titled A History of Bermuda and Its Paper Money. *Imagine the surprise those numismatic enthusiasts will get when they come across this title by Nelson Aspen!*

Fruity Waldorf Salad

No jokes about the name. And no, for any of you that may have run into me there, I didn't pick up this recipe at Peter Allen's 1986 birthday bash at the Waldorf-Astoria, either. I was way too busy workin' the room to worry about food!

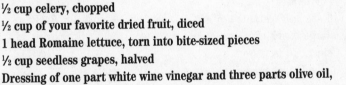

4 cups green apples, chopped
½ cup lemon juice
⅔ cup slivered almonds
½ cup celery, chopped
½ cup of your favorite dried fruit, diced
1 head Romaine lettuce, torn into bite-sized pieces
½ cup seedless grapes, halved
Dressing of one part white wine vinegar and three parts olive oil,
**   seasoned to taste**

Toss your apples in the lemon juice, then stir in everything else except the dressing. Please make sure you tear the lettuce into manageable pieces. There's nothing worse than seeing someone trying to cram one big piece into her mouth all at once. And if you don't have a salad spinner, use paper towels to pat the lettuce dry. If you saw Suzanne Pleshette play Leona Helmsley in the TV biopic, you know how wet lettuce can lead to Armaggedon! Refrigerate for at least 2 hours.

Drizzle the oil and vinegar mixture lightly over the top and toss again before serving. Those of you with kids will want to serve this one when my pals the Wiggles come for dinner . . . you know how they love fruit salads!

Green Goddess Soup

Since we're supposed to get 5 servings of fruits and vegetables daily, this incredibly savory soup will more than meet your recommended daily allowance. I like it piping hot, but you can also opt for serving it chilled during those sweltering summer months.

1 onion, chopped
1 large potato, peeled and chopped
2 tablespoons olive oil
3 bunches of fresh asparagus, ends snapped off and cut in 1-inch pieces
½ cup water
16 ounces vegetable broth
1 large bunch of fresh spinach
Celery salt to taste
Ground black pepper to taste
Low-fat or fat-free sour cream for garnish
Minced onions for garnish

Sauté the onion and potato in the olive oil over medium heat until the onion is soft, about 5 minutes. Add asparagus pieces and continue until they turn bright in color, about 3 minutes. Then add your water and broth. Bring to a boil, then reduce heat and simmer for 20 minutes.

Remove from the stove and puree your mixture in the blender in batches. As you puree each batch, transfer it into a second pot. When finished, ladle the smooth mixture back into the blender one batch at a time, and puree again, each time adding some spinach to the mix. After all the spinach is added, put it all back into the original soup pot.

Boil the pureed batch, then reduce to a simmer while you salt and pepper to taste.

Serve garnished with a dollop of sour cream and a sprinkling of minced onions. Mmmmm! Your guests will be green with envy until you share the recipe, and if you do, you will be a god or goddess!

Fem-Bot's Fried Cabbage with Bacon and Onion

Gorgeous Cindy Margolis, "the most downloaded woman on the Internet," is known best for her sexy swimsuit spreads and as one of the luscious and lethal fem-bots in the original *Austin Powers* movie. She's also a real sweetheart and one of the most generous and enterprising businesswomen in Hollywood. Her husband, Guy Starkman, owns Jerry's Famous Deli, so she's not one of those glamour girls who's afraid to tuck in to a hearty meal! Here's one of her guilty pleasures she shared with me. It makes a very tasty side dish . . . especially if you're grilling up some succulent brats!

5 thick slices of bacon
2 tablespoons butter
1 small white onion, sliced very thin
1 small head of cabbage, cut in half
1 bay leaf
Water
2 tablespoons cider vinegar
Black pepper

Cut bacon into one-inch pieces and place in large frying pan over medium heat. Cook until ready to turn, then add butter and onion. Turn slices and continue frying. As the onions brown, add cut cabbage halves and bay leaf.

Gradually add just enough water to cover the cabbage. Allow to come to a boil, stirring often to help loosen the brown bits in the pan. Cook 15 to 20 minutes to desired tenderness.

Stir in vinegar and heat an additional 5 minutes. Sprinkle with coarse black pepper just before serving.

And what's more, baby, she can cook!!

Great Grape-Mint Sorbet

Sure, it cleanses the palate and could even be considered a dessert, but this easy and pretty little creation is another opportunity to show off how much attention you like to give to details. Another super idea to experiment with.

8 large grapefruits, peeled
Fresh mint leaves to taste
¾ cup powdered sugar

Mix the three ingredients in a blender or food processor until smooth. Freeze until just past slushy. The consistency will vary, depending on how cold your freezer temperature runs, so try it out sometime before the big night.

Voilà, Sorbet!

Serve delicate portions in your showiest martini glasses, garnished with a fresh mint leaf.

MAIN COURSE

The big event! There must be some of the Italian mama in me, because there's nothing I like more than entering the dining room with an enormous, steaming bowl or platter of the entrée. Eating "family style" is my preferred method of serving, since it really creates a holiday atmosphere (without all those pesky real-life family issues). Of course, if you're making a more elaborate presentation, it's best to prepare the plates individually in the seclusion of your kitchen.

Do everyone a favor and wash your hands frequently during food preparation. Don't be a spendthrift: Use paper towels freely, since dishcloths hold on to germs. Try not to think about the fact that Valerie Perrine wears little gloves when she reads the newspaper to avoid dirtying her lovely fingers. She believes that one's hands age with every washing. I wonder if she wears gloves when cooking!

Offer fresh ground black pepper, sea salt, and red pepper flakes so everyone can control the temperatures of their meal. Some people won't be able to taste your efforts if they've seared off their sensitive taste buds.

There may never be a resolution to the debate over prayer in school, nor is there an easy answer for how to handle it at the dinner table. Sadly, the notion of bowing your head in thanks seems to make today's cosmopolitan diners amazingly uncomfortable. I do, however, like to acknowledge the gift of friends gathered in bounty before everyone attacks the food. This is best accomplished with a thank-you to the guests and a toast. Don't feel guilty if you don't utter the G-word. He knows what you're thinking, after all. Oh, and as for those toasts—the clinking of glasses, aside from being murder on Waterford, is an acquired habit of modern society. It's really all about eye contact and the intent of the salute, not the *ting-a-ling* of your crystal.

> *Stuck for a blessing to satisfy all denominations? "Love wholeheartedly, be surprised, give thanks, and praise. Then you will discover the fullness of your life."* —BROTHER DAVID STEINDL-RAST

A word about side dishes: simplicity. Your featured entrée should be the star attraction and side dishes, the supporting cast. Besides, vegetables and starches taste so divine prepared without fuss. Steam some spinach or boil little red potatoes. Add a squirt of fresh lemon or a sprinkle of garlic salt and you're all set. If you're feeling fancy, make a little Krispy Korean Kole-Slaw (see previous chapter), which is really all smoke and no fire.

Subliminally seduce your sexiest dinner guest by making sure to lock eyes directly with him/her during a toast. If an unbroken gaze is returned, so is the desire! More powerful than the Magic Eight Ball!

Dig in, and talk, talk, talk! Maybe you'll find out which soap studs are dating each other. *Oh, that explains why he was killed off so suddenly!* People eat at different paces, so don't be in a rush to clear away plates before everyone has finished. As host, try not to jump up from the table too often unless it's to replenish the wine supply. Constantly leaping out of your seat to retrieve something from the kitchen will only unnerve your guests. Besides, you'll never get more than a mouthful of food that isn't room temperature! After all, the more content, relaxed, and comfortable *you* are, the more you'll pass those feelings on to the rest of the gang gathered around you.

"That which chiefly causes the failure of a dinner party, is the running short—not of meat, nor yet of drink, but of conversation."
—LEWIS CARROLL (1832–1898)

Scrumptious Shrimp Curry

2 pounds fresh shrimp, peeled and deveined
½ cup olive oil
2 teaspoons curry powder
3 peppers (red, yellow, green), chopped
1 large red onion, diced
¼ cup brandy
⅓ cup teriyaki sauce
2 cups cooked rice

Flirt with your fishmonger and buy the largest, freshest shrimp he has available at the market. It never hurts to bat your eyelashes and ask if anything has recently come in other than what's already on display. When you get them home, clean well by washing and deveining. Saute in ¼ cup olive oil just until the shrimp is pink, about 3 to 5 minutes, sprinkling in 1 tablespoon of curry powder. Remove from skillet.

In the same skillet, use the remaining oil to sauté the peppers, onion, and the remaining curry powder. As soon as the peppers begin to soften (about 5 minutes), add the brandy, teriyaki, and shrimp. Cook until everything is well heated and stir often to keep from burning. Serve quickly over white or saffron rice.

What about the age-old dilemma of whether or not to leave the tails on the shrimp? Personally, I don't like to handle food with my fingers when I can use a fork, and not everyone has the dainty little forks so perfect for seafood. That's why I pinch the tails off the shrimp beforehand. I vote for making it easier on those dining and saving yourself the distasteful sight of seeing Sam or Sarah suck the last bit of succulent shrimp from the tail portion, clenched between thumb and forefinger. If you do opt to leave the tails on, be sure to have finger bowls as part of each place setting.

The Lord Is My Shepherd's Pie

A non-denominational dish that is sure to delight!

Back when *Melrose Place* was the preferred way to while away a Monday night,* my gal pal Pam and I used to make this delicious sure-fire fare to share with friends, gathered around the TV set. It's a great way to make use of leftovers, too, and you can throw just about any of your favorite savories into this casserole, the king of comfort food! Whether your vegetables are fresh or frozen, either way, you can't go wrong.

Pam turned me on to the most wonderful, savory relish from the United Kingdom called Branston's Pickle . . . sort of a brown chutney and pure heaven. If you can manage to find it in a specialty shoppe or have traveling friends bring you back a few jars, it's a smashing complement to the mashed potatoes and a welcome addition to any "knees up" (that's Cockney slang for a "festive celebration")!

---

*Can't you still hear the synthesized guitar riff of the theme song? Who wants reality TV if you're old enough to remember Amanda vs. Allison? Krystal vs. Alexis? Neely vs. Helen? Margo vs. Eve? You'll be relieved to know, still gorgeous Gordon Thomson ("Adam Carrington") assured me that Linda Evans and Joan Collins lived up to their on-screen personae of Darling and Diva!

2 pounds ground beef or turkey
½ cup hot salsa
2 teaspoons Worcestershire sauce
1 tablespoon garlic salt
1 teaspoon pepper
½ cup onions, chopped
1 cup frozen peas
1 cup carrots, sliced
1 cup frozen green beans
32-ounce can fat-free baked beans
32-ounce can kidney beans, drained
6 large potatoes
½ cup skim milk
½ cup butter
2 tablespoons minced garlic
1 teaspoon pepper
1 tablespoon garlic salt
2 cups Cheddar cheese, shredded
Branston's Pickle or similar relish/chutney to taste

Preheat your oven to 350 degrees. Saute the ground beef until no longer pink, about 5 minutes. Drain excess oil, then add in the salsa and Worcestershire sauce, salt, pepper, and chopped onions. Remove from heat and mix in the peas, carrots, and beans.

Boil the potatoes until tender, about 15 to 20 minutes, then mash them with the milk, butter, and garlic. Salt to taste. We like ours lumpy. The consistency is up to you, but avoid overworking them.

Place the beef mixture into a baking dish, then spread the mashed potatoes on top. Bake at 350 degrees for 40 minutes. Sprinkle some shredded Cheddar cheese over the top and continue to bake for 5 to 10 more minutes or until the pie begins to bubble.

Topping it off with a hearty dollop of Branston's or pickled dressing is brilliant!

Titanic Turkey Meat Loaf from a Re-Past Life

Nothing takes you back to your childhood (or in my case, *someone else's*!) like the comforting heartiness of a meatloaf. I like using ground turkey even better than sirloin or hamburger meat. Just pressing the mixture into the loaf pan is as therapeutic as a past life regression! I should know—I believe I'm reincarnated from one Milton C. Long, a first class passenger on the ill-fated *Titanic* (which could explain my unnatural obsession with doomed ocean liners and general aversion to iceberg lettuce). Follow this recipe and there's no way your dinner will founder!

4 egg whites, lightly beaten
4 garlic cloves, minced
1½ teaspoons dried basil
1 teaspoon dried rosemary
1 teaspoon salt
½ teaspoon crushed red pepper
1 large green apple, peeled, cored, and finely chopped
1 cup onions, chopped
1 cup bread crumbs
2 pounds ground turkey
1¼ cup tomato paste
Cooking spray
Grated Parmesan, to taste
Optional: olive oil, Tabasco, scallions, to taste

Preheat the oven to 350 degrees, then stir together the egg whites, garlic, basil, rosemary, salt, and red pepper. Once mixed, add the finely chopped apple, onions, and bread crumbs. Finally, add the turkey and combine, being careful not to over mix. It is not necessary to cook the turkey beforehand, but I do like to quickly sauté it with a touch of olive oil, Tabasco, and minced scallions, then pour off any excess fat.

Did you know I had a bit part in the biggest box office Turkey of all time, Ishtar? A few shots of me in the final scene survived the cutting room floor. Look for (a very young) Nelson as an army private in the nightclub finale scene. Now that was acting!

Put your mixture into a loaf pan sprayed with cooking spray and bake for 15 minutes. "Paint" the tomato paste over the loaf and return to the oven for another 25 to 30 minutes. Let stand for 5 minutes before slicing and sprinkling with Parmesan.

If there's any left over, gobble gobble it up cold as a late-night snack or luncheon sandwich.

A tricky tip if you happen to come across a forgotten can of cranberry sauce from last Thanksgiving: use the same amount of cranberry sauce, instead of the tomato paste. It makes for a sweeter, holiday version. As Captain E. J. Smith commanded his crew, "Be British!" and pass it to the "women and children first!"

"After dinner I was enjoying a cup of coffee, when a man about twenty-eight or thirty years of age drew up, and introduced himself as Milton C. Long. . . . He was traveling alone. We talked together for an hour or so." —JOHN "JACK" THAYER, *Titanic* SURVIVOR

Sirloin Steaks: The Manly Meal

I rarely indulge in red meat, but every now and then Dad comes to town. Here's a simple, delicious recipe to serve four carnivores since, if you're like me, you probably don't know more than that.

The consolation, I tell myself, is what my actress friend Carol Lynley advised me at a *Poseidon Adventure* banquet: "I try to eat red meat twice a year. It keeps me aggressive."

4 six-ounce sirloin steaks
8 tablespoons butter
4 chopped shallots
1 tablespoon Worcestershire sauce
Salt and pepper, to taste
Fresh parsley, minced, to taste

Heat 2 tablespoons of the butter in a saucepan over medium heat. Add the shallots and sauté until they begin to brown.

Next, add the 1 tablespoon of Worcestershire and heat until the sauce starts to bubble. If you like, pass the time trying to remember all the lyrics to *The Morning After*. It won the Oscar for Best Original Song from a Motion Picture in 1972.

Add six tablespoons butter to a second skillet and cook for about 3 to 5 minutes over medium heat. Then add your steaks and cook for about 4 minutes on each side. Vary the cooking time depending on your taste.

Sprinkle some salt and lots of coarse black pepper on top of the steaks, then serve with the shallot sauce poured over and sprinkled with minced parsley.

Did you know Carol Lynley's grandfather was a butcher? You should see this gorgeous Award-winning actress carve a turkey! Rent Once You Kiss a Stranger *and you'll get the idea. She can wield a mean harpoon, too!*

Cancer the Crab Cakes
(The Kind of Crabs You Won't Mind Having!)

Born July 1, I am a *true* Cancerian—ruled by the moon and sentimental, a homebody, moody. I used to share my special day with the beloved Lady Di, but now there's only Pamela Anderson and Olivia de Havilland left to compete with. Of course, while Diana will be forever 36 and perpetually stunning, the rest of us have to keep up with the microdermabrasion, glycolic acid antioxidant treatments and slathering on the sunscreen.

This one takes some lead time, so plan ahead. Now blow out the candles and make a wish!

12 ounces cooked
   crab meat
2 eggs, lightly beaten
4 tablespoons onion,
   finely chopped
4 tablespoons low-fat
   or fat-free mayonnaise
2 tablespoons fresh parsley, chopped
4 tablespoons dijon mustard
4 teaspoons fresh thyme
2 teaspoons Worcestershire sauce
Salt, to taste

1 cup fine dry bread crumbs
½ cup cornmeal
4 tablespoons olive oil
Lemon wedges for garnish
Cayenne pepper and extra mayo, to taste

In a large bowl, combine eggs, onion, mayo, parsley, mustard, thyme, Worcestershire, a pinch of salt, and half of your bread crumbs. Stir in the crab, mixing well.

Shape mixture into eight patties, about ¾ inch thick.

Combine the remaining bread crumbs and cornmeal, then coat the patties with this mixture. Refrigerate in wax paper for a day or two.

In a large skillet, heat your oil and cook those crabbies over medium heat. Three minutes on each side is recommended . . . they will be golden and aromatic.

Serve 'em right away with a spicy tartar sauce made of cayenne pepper and mayonnaise. Put a fat lemon wedge on the side and enjoy!

Hmm . . . I wonder what that hunky Tyler Florence's sign is! I'm *certain* it must be compatible with mine.

Sometimes a matter of perspective is all it takes to avert a dinner party disaster. There was an outdoor birthday party I attended in Malibu in honor of my dear longtime pal Amy. Just as her main course was being served, a clumsy seagull dropped a live, flopping fish right onto her plate! We all shrieked, aghast, and the bloody fish floundered all over the table, sending food flying. An older woman seated nearby didn't bat an eyelash, but instead commented with bemusement, "That's good luck, honey. It means you're gonna meet a Pisces." That's the spirit of keeping your glass half full!

Salmon Patties (Not Sam and Patty's)

This is the sister dish to the Crab Cakes. You can grill these and serve them on hamburger buns at your next BBQ, or dress them up with relish and garnish to make a tasty main course. They're best made fresh, but can also be frozen and cooked later (within 1 to 2 weeks). This recipe will make 8 large patties.

2 to 3 pounds fresh salmon fillet
¾ cup dry bread crumbs
1 large egg, beaten
1 large onion, finely chopped
3 tablespoons fresh dill, finely chopped
Juice and zest of one lemon
1 shallot, minced
2 tablespoons olive oil
1½ teaspoons red wine vinegar
Salt and pepper to taste

Chop the fish with your sharpest knife until it is the consistency of lump crab, or place pieces in the food processor for a few pulses. Be sure not to overdo it . . . you want the meat of the fish to remain chunky!

Add each ingredient one at a time until all are combined. Form the patties just as you would hamburgers, but not too thick to ensure even cooking.

Fry them up in a lightly oiled skillet, turning only once. A mango chutney or dijon mustard are both delicious toppings for these pretty patties!

Perfect Paella

Paella (*paa ay aa*) is a Spanish delight whose name comes from melding the nineteenth-century Latin words *patella*, "small dish," and *patina* "shallow dish."

This is one of my favorite dishes to make when it's a romantic evening for two, or to share with friends on a celebratory evening like New Year's Eve or someone's birthday. It's easy to adjust for vegetarians and well loved by almost everyone. When cooking with shellfish, always buy the freshest, cleanest available (befriend your fishmonger!), and be sure to ascertain that none of your guests suffer from food allergies. Having paramedics drop in to your dinner party can really *taint* the evening. Also consider that some people in L.A. are buying into the strange "chickens as pets" craze, so ensure that none of them are on your guest list!

This particular recipe will serve 8 very hungry people. Be sure to go light on the appetizers!

1 pound fresh clams
1 pound fresh oysters
4 skinless chicken breasts
⅔ cup olive oil
1 large onion, minced
¼ cup fresh parsley, chopped
4 garlic cloves, peeled and crushed
¼ teaspoon saffron
1 16-ounce can low-fat, low-sodium chicken broth
6 green and/or red peppers, sliced
16 ounces tomato sauce
2 teaspoons sugar
8 cups rice
14 cups water
1½ pounds shrimp
1 pound scallops
Salt, to taste

Steam the clams and oysters in a large pot until they open (about 5 to 7 minutes).

Meanwhile, dice chicken breasts into chunks. In a skillet, sauté onion, parsley, and garlic in olive oil over medium heat until onions are translucent. Add saffron, broth, peppers and chicken and simmer until chicken is cooked, approximately 7-8 min.

Transfer this mixture into the pot. Stir in tomato sauce and sugar. Add your rice and water and bring to a boil for five full minutes, stirring occasionally.

Add shrimp and scallops, reduce to a simmer for 5 minutes, stirring occasionally. Their aromas will soon fill the entire house. Take your steamed clams and oysters and add to this wonderful mixture. This is one occasion when you can keep the tails on the shrimp and the clams and oysters in their shells. Just make sure you have plenty of napkins on hand. Finger bowls would be a smart addition to your table setting.

Reduce heat, cover, and let simmer for 10 minutes or until all the water is absorbed. Give it one good stir and serve with pitchers of strong sangria (see Beverages) and say, "Holy Toledo!" Antonio Banderas isn't the only Spanish dish in Hollywood!

Self-effacing Academy Award winner Catherine Zeta-Jones, on being just a "kid from Wales," said, "At least I know which forks to use when I'm at the U.N." Will you?!

Cross-Country Chicken Fried Steak

When I "loaded up the Chevy and moved to Bever-lee" from the Big Apple, my best friend Glenn came along with me for the not-very-comfortable ride in a little Chevy Sprint that would have lost out in a race with a push mower! We spent five days and 3,000 miles in motels that would have terrified Alfred Hitchcock and logged a grand total of about five minutes looking at the Grand Canyon. It's not as conveniently located from the main highway as the map would lead one to believe. We also made prolonged and ultimately vain attempts at getting him to learn the *Just in Love* duet from the Broadway musical *Call Me Madam*. It was a wise decision for him to pursue a Wall Street career rather than one on the stage. Regardless, it was a positive bonding experience for us, and how else would we ever have come to visit the tiny town of Shamrock, Texas?

Finding a relatively clean and friendly place to stop for dinner was a nightly challenge and we dined more than once on that delicious staple of Southern cuisine, Chicken Fried Steak, so named because it is steak fried like a piece of chicken, then slathered with a lumpy, creamy, and admittedly delicious poor, white gravy.

I've tried many different versions of this hearty dish, which I like to serve with lumpy, creamy and admittedly delicious poor, white mashed potatoes (throw in a tablespoon of horseradish for a real boost!). Here's the way I like it best, followed by the instructions for that gravy! This serves eight *very* hungry travelers.

8 medium-sized (12 ounces) sirloin steaks, thinly cut
4 teaspoons salt
6 teaspoons black pepper
2 teaspoons cayenne pepper
4 teaspoons garlic powder
4 cups flour
4 eggs
2 cups buttermilk
4 cups salted crackers, crumbled
Approximately 2 cups vegetable oil

Season the meat with the salt, pepper, cayenne, and garlic powder and tenderize with a mallet. It's fun to get out your aggression by doing your best Judge Judy impression and hammering those suckers until you pronounce them "Tender!"

Have three bowls ready: one with flour, one with milk and eggs combined, and one with the cracker crumbs. Coat each piece of meat evenly with flour (shaking off excess), then dredge into liquid, followed by the crumbs. Set aside until all are completed.

Heat oil in your skillet over medium heat. When hot, add steaks. Make sure you're not wearing your best checkered gingham ensemble, because it will spatter. Make sure the oil covers the meat no more than halfway. When the inner juices of the meat begin to seep through the crusted mixture on top, you will know it is time to turn it over. An important note: Every recipe I've found for this stresses that the success of your pan-frying relies on only turning the steak *once* during the process. It's easier to gauge by the look of the meat itself than by time, but cook the meat approximately 5 minutes on each side.

Remove cooked steaks from the pan and place on paper towels. You may keep them warm in a 200-degree oven while you whisk up the gravy.

6 tablespoons flour
About 4 tablespoons oil from the skillet
1½ cups chicken or beef stock
1½ cups cream
4 teaspoons salt
4 teaspoons coarse black pepper

In the same skillet, now drained of all but a few tablespoons of the oil, turn up just slightly and add in the flour. Stir until pasty. No, Eddy, I said "Pasty!" A lump or two will only add authenticity and character to the final product.

Whisk in the stock and let the mixture begin to thicken and bubble. As you gradually add the cream, also make sure to keep stirring in the brown bits formed on the bottom of the skillet . . . this will add tremendous flavor. Of course, add lots and lots of salt and black pepper.

American Dining Slang, you never know when it might come in handy!

- *In the alley = serve as a side dish*
- *Bucket of cold mud = a serving of chocolate ice cream*
- *Two cows, make 'em cry = two hamburgers with onions*
- *On a raft = served on toast*
- *Eve with a lid on = apple pie*

Nelson's Big, Succulent Coq au Vin

Hey, simmer down now. Wayy down! 'Cause it's the simmering that's the key to this classic French dish hearty enough to satisfy any size queen. You'll be so proud of the way this one turns out, the cock won't be the only one crowing!

6 slices of bacon, chopped
1 cup onions, chopped
1 pound mushrooms, sliced
¼ cup butter (optional, but so good!)
1 4-pound chicken, cut up: breasts, legs, thighs
4 cups chicken stock (canned broth is fine)
2 cups red wine
4 tablespoons hot mustard
1 teaspoon thyme
¼ teaspoon paprika
2 bay leaves
2 tablespoons cornstarch
Salt and ground black pepper, to taste

You may want to use breast meat only, but I find the variety of the poultry makes the overall dish more delish. I do remove the skin and wash the meat, separating the parts before I begin.

Over medium heat in a large pan, render your bacon, then the onions and mushrooms, cooking until browned. If you're not getting enough liquid from the bacon, add the butter. Oh, what the hell . . . add it anyway. It's so French!

Next, in goes the chicken followed by the stock and the wine. Whisk in the mustard with a fork. Stir the mixture often for 2 to 3 minutes before adding the remaining seasonings. As soon as this aromatic concoction starts to bubble, cover the pan and reduce heat to a simmer for at least 30 minutes, up to an hour.

The meat will have begun to detach from the bone, which means you can be cocksure of your success! Remove the chicken and set it aside while you follow the next steps.

Return the heat to high. While the sauce returns to a boil, mix up a few tablespoons of room temperature water with your cornstarch in a little bowl, then add it into the vegetables and liquid. Continue boiling while it thickens (won't take long), then add salt and/or pepper to taste.

You can pour this *fantastique* sauce over the chicken in individual serving bowls or make a spectacular presentation by putting everything together in one giant bowl to present to your guests. Serve with gorgeous little boiled red potatoes sprinkled with thyme and lots of crusty French bread.

Some thoughtful hosts remove the bay leaves prior to serving their guests, but I always get a kick out of seeing how someone handles the surprise of having a whole one suddenly lodged against the roof of their mouth. Just kidding!

cockalorum (kah-kuh-LOR-um). *noun. A boastful and self-important person, a boastful talk*

Secret Agent Spinach Strata

Here's a dish my Big Fat Greek Uncle Leo from Athens would have loved. It's a great menu choice if you're having multiple guests with differing tastes. Suppose you were to have all your agents, managers, editors, and life coaches over at the same time. Mark hates mayo and butter . . . Jeremie loves goat cheese . . . and anything with curry is out for Maura. John is easy ("Agents are sharks: we eat *anything*!") and Tinker will scrutinize the fat content per serving. Well, this lasagna-like crowd-pleaser (*strata* means "layers") should suit everyone to a T for Ten percent!

1 pound ground chorizo sausage
1 sweet yellow bell pepper, sliced
8 to 10 ounces fresh spinach, chopped
6 eggs
1½ cups milk
½ teaspoon kosher salt
½ teaspoon coarse black pepper
¼ teaspoon nutmeg
Cooking spray
Up to a dozen slices of hearty baguettes
1½ cups jack cheese, shredded
1 cup feta cheese

In a large skillet, sauté the ground sausage until cooked, about 10 minutes. Remove to a separate bowl, then sauté the sliced pepper and chopped spinach in whatever fat remains in the skillet. Drain, then combine vegetables with the sausage in the bowl.

Add eggs, milk, salt, pepper, and nutmeg to the contents of the bowl, mixing thoroughly with a spoon.

Spray a baking dish with non-stick spray and arrange slices of your baguette in an overlapping pattern (think of that lovely lattice work in a Greek garden!). Spoon the mixture on top of the bread. Next, crumble on the Jack and feta cheeses until your bread is entirely covered.

Pop the dish, covered, into the refrigerator overnight or for several hours. A half hour before you're ready to bake, remove from fridge and preheat oven to 350 degrees. Bake about 40 minutes; you will notice it browning to perfection.

Simple, Super Salmon Penne

A note on cooking pasta: Fresh pasta takes 3 minutes or less to cook in about 6 quarts of salted water at a full rolling boil. Commercial dried pasta, about 6 to 8 minutes. To test, take a bite and make sure it's *al dente*, somewhat firm to the bite. A drop of olive oil in the water or a hearty dash of kosher salt will keep your pasta from sticking. I like to rinse cooked pasta in warm water to remove starch and prevent it from over cooking, but my Aunt Rita doesn't like to rinse at all, believing that the starch helps to hold the sauce to the noodle.

This one is fattening, make no mistake. And if you're not a penne fan, choose another hearty noodle like pappardelle or farfalla. When I want to cut corners (and save on fat and calories), I don't make the sauce from scratch . . . I use a store-bought fat-free alfredo sauce. There. I admitted it.

2 good-sized filleted salmon steaks (12 ounces each)
3 cups heavy cream
1 cup fresh basil leaves, chopped
8 ounces fresh grated Parmesan
2 16-ounce boxes of penne
2 tablespoons olive oil
4 tablespoons capers
½ cup frozen peas
2 tablespoons garlic, minced
½ cup onions, chopped
½ cup sun-dried tomatoes
2 tablespoons garlic, minced
2 glasses Pinot Grigio
6 ounces grated Gruyère cheese
Tabasco, to taste
Salsa, to taste

Bake salmon steaks at 450 degrees for 10 minutes on each side, then flake the meat into a bowl.

Meanwhile, bring the cream to a boil in a saucepan. Reduce heat and simmer until thick (about 25 minutes). Add basil and 6 ounces of grated Parmesan. As soon as the cheese melts, remove the saucepan from the heat.

Bring 10 to 12 quarts of water to a rolling boil for the pasta. Make 2 boxes (16 servings), since you're feeding eight big appetites. You want the portions to be enormous!

Quickly sauté the capers, peas, garlic, onions and sun-dried tomatoes in olive oil until the onions are translucent, then add one glass of wine. Add this mixture to the cream sauce and return to the stove over low heat.

As the sauce begins to bubble, you can add the Gruyére, a shot or two of Tabasco, and the salsa to "pinken" its color. At this point, pour the second glass of wine and reward yourself for a few minutes.

Keep the heat on the sauce to low and when the pasta is cooked and draining in the colander, add the flaked salmon and mix well with a wooden spoon. Your mouth, by now, is watering.

Ladle that creamy, steaming sauce over the pasta in the largest serving bowl you have and top with the remaining grated Parmesan.

And then, Mama Mia, Dancing Queen! Make your entrance!

Arrabiata Sauce

"In dinner talk, it is perhaps allowable to fling any faggot rather than let the fire go out." —J. M. BARRIE (1860–1937)

This zesty sauce has its own personality and is wonderful over hearty, fat noodles like ziti, penne, or rigatoni. It's also great for lasagna, and it freezes well. Mine is a vegetarian version, but the spicy, robust flavor enhances smoked chicken, pork, pepperoni, turkey, or good old meatballs. (When's the last time you had a meatball sandwich? Even if you're not from South Philly, treat yourself tomorrow at lunch!)

16 Romano tomatoes, peeled (or two 24-ounce cans with juice)
½ cup olive oil
4 teaspoons garlic, minced
2 teaspoons fresh oregano
3 small fresh jalapeño peppers, finely chopped
¼ cup sun-dried tomatoes
2 tablespoons capers
2 tablespoons black olive slices
Parmesan cheese, grated

If using fresh tomatoes, cut them into quarters and remove seeds. In a large skillet over medium heat, sauté the other ingredients in olive oil for about four minutes, then add tomatoes.

Continue for another minute or two until the tomatoes are soft but still holding their shape. Salt and pepper to taste, then sprinkle with grated Parmesan and serve very hot. Quick and easy . . . just like some of my best friends.

Low-Fat Pasta Chicken Bake

The ingredients for this really depend on what you have on hand. My former in-laws and friends back in South Dakota call this kind of dish "Shipwreck," and their version includes any-and-all leftovers, covered with canned Cream of Mushroom Soup and baked with a Velveeta and potato chip crust. My methods are just as simple, but a whole lot healthier. This is really low-fat and shamefully easy. Don't ever let anyone see you prepare it, or your cover is blown.

4 large boneless, skinless chicken breasts, cut into chunks
2 tablespoons olive oil
2 medium-sized yellow squash, sliced
2 medium-sized zucchini, sliced
½ cup onions, chopped
½ cup carrots, sliced
1 bottle of fat-free Italian salad dressing
1 16-ounce box of rotelli (or other curly) pasta
Salt and pepper, to taste
1 package of low-fat or fat-free cheese (mozzarella or cheddar)

Preheat the oven to 350 degrees. In a large skillet, sauté the chicken in oil over medium heat for about 5 to 7 minutes, until the meat is no longer pink. Add the squash, zucchini, onions, and carrots. Give them a stir for another 2 minutes, then pour in the salad dressing. When thoroughly mixed, remove to a large bowl.

Cook pasta at a rolling boil per package instructions. Rinse and drain it, then add to the chicken and vegetables and stir well. Add salt and pepper, to taste.

Spray a lasagna pan with non-fat, no-stick cooking spray and spread the mixture inside, topping with the cheese. Bake for 45 minutes or until cheese is bubbly. Serves 6 to 8. Gilligan and the castaways never had a shipwreck so good!

Did you know? There are more chickens in the world than there are people. Go ahead and have seconds!

Chicken? Dump Him, Dumpling!

Is your man giving you trouble? Don't be a chicken...lose him, pronto! Life's too short, and while you're recovering you can indulge in this lip-smacking comfort food. Maybe you're the dump-ee...an even better excuse to whip up this rib-sticking recipe. Just don't be bitter: Consider being dumped a roundabout way of being introduced to your *next* boyfriend!

> *"One of the most time-consuming things is to have an enemy."*
> —E. B. WHITE

1 whole 5-pound chicken
2 onions, chopped
1 bunch celery, chopped
5 carrots, chopped
1 tablespoon ground peppercorns
1 teaspoon thyme, chopped
1 bay leaf
2 cloves, crushed

Place the whole bird in a large pot and cover with water. Bring to a boil. If you saved the giblets, you may clean, chop and add these. (If you do, skip the liver. It has a strong taste and will greatly darken the color of your mixture.) Stir in onions, celery, and carrots along with the peppercorns, thyme, bay leaf, and cloves. Continue stirring until mixture returns to a boil.

Cover pot, reduce heat, and simmer for two hours (or even longer if you like) until the chicken is tender and the meat begins to loosen from the carcass. Check from time to time, adding water if necessary.

Remove from heat, skim off the fat from the surface. Remove the bird and discard its skin and bones. Slice and dice the tender, juicy meat and strain your stock. Back into the pot go the stock and meat . . . return to low heat, and it's time to make the dumplings.

Of course, since short cuts leave more time for sipping wine, you can always just follow the directions on the side of the Bisquik box!

For the dumplings:

1½ cup flour
2 teaspoons baking powder
½ teaspoon salt
1 tablespoon shortening
¾ cup milk
¼ cup grated Parmesan

Thoroughly mix flour, baking powder, and salt. Blend in shortening and add milk. Drop by tablespoons right into the gently simmering stock. Cover for about 15 minutes. Add ¼ cup grated parmesan cheese and/or 3 tbsp. finely chopped parsley if desired.

Indulge in this delicious meal, then start scanning the personal ads! Look at it this way, no more summer vacations stuck on a pontoon boat with his relatives.

"His mother should have thrown him away and kept the stork."
—MAE WEST

Perfectly Planned Pomegranate Pork Medallions

My lovely friend Chris Barrett personifies simple elegance when it comes to interior design. Her "less is more" approach to decor has worked for high-end clients from Richard Dean Anderson to Charlize Theron. That principle can also be applied to designing a dinner plate. Don't overwhelm your guests with a big, overdone production when a simple presentation, like this one from her recipe files that will serve 4, says so much more.

Note: Like Chris, I find that to make the demi-glace required for this dish (that smooth, savory brown glaze, made from an intense reduction of meaty flavors) is extremely labor intensive, so save yourself the time and aggravation and buy it pre-made.

4 pounds pork loin fillets
Salt and pepper, to taste
⅔ cup butter
1 cup demi-glace
1 cup pomegranate juice
4 tablespoons fresh, minced parsley

Trim the tips from the pork fillets and remove excess fat and filament. Cut them into 1-inch-thick pieces and season lightly with salt and pepper.

Over medium heat, melt half the butter in a 12-inch skillet. When hot, add the pork and sauté about 5 minutes each side ensuring thorough cooking. Don't, however, let the meat dry out. Remove and keep warm on a plate, covered loosely with aluminum foil.

Deglaze the skillet with demi-glace and pomegranate juice, being sure to scrape all the browned bits into the sauce. Reduce over high heat for approximately 2 minutes, until thickened.

Lower the heat and whisk remaining butter into the sauce, seasoning with additional salt and pepper.

Spoon this over the center of a warmed dinner plate, then place the pork fillets on top. Sprinkle the dish with minced parsley and serve with tantalizingly tasty new potatoes and steamed green beans.

Mmm . . . A delicious design for dining!

Chasen's Famous Chili

Every movie buff knows that David Chasen's famous Beverly Hills restaurant was best known for its coveted chili recipe . . . so enticing that Elizabeth Taylor was rumored to have batches of it shipped all the way to Rome when she was filming *Cleopatra*. Of course, judging by the photographs of her when she was living in Virginia as wife to Senator John Warner, maybe there were some other times when fattening foods were being delivered by express mail. (I happen to know that during her frequent hospital stays, she loves to order in specialty pizzas! Sure beats lime gelatin!)

It was a sad day when Chasen's closed its doors to be renovated into a high-end supermarket* (I got in one last meal there, accompanied by my gorgeous actress friend Mary Kay Adams—*The Guiding Light*'s "India von Halkein Spaulding" and "Grilka" on *Star Trek: Deep Space Nine*), and we took photographs like starstruck tourists! How many Tinseltown legends had eaten at that banquette, we wondered. Only the ghosts of Jimmy Stewart, Norma

---

*Chasen's briefly resurfaced at a new location but paled in comparison to the original, as did the chili. The revamp became known primarily as a stop on the blue-haired-ladies-who-lunch circuit, although I did have a memorable luncheon there with the chain-smoking Frank Gorshin, known as the better "Riddler" on TV's *Batman*. And there was the time Farrah Fawcett literally fell into former manager Jay Bernstein's engagement party with a bandaged arm. That was a pretty good party that lasted only slightly less time than the subsequent marriage. It was there that I became friends with the great Gloria Allred. I couldn't help noticing how unusually small her feet are and, after a couple glasses of champagne, I had to remark upon it. "Yes, but they kick big butt!" she quipped, flashing her sexy, sly smile. I now sleep much better knowing her business card is in my Rolodex; if she can win a suit against Aaron Spelling, she can protect *any* underdog!

Shearer, and Douglas Fairbanks know! But at least they allowed this winning recipe to be revealed at long last.

The master chef would make an enormous batch every Sunday, then freeze it for the week since he believed its best taste came through when reheated. Try it yourself and have a taste of Hollywood history!

½ pound dried pinto beans
1 28-ounce can diced tomatoes in juice
1 large green bell pepper, chopped
2 tablespoons vegetable oil
3 cups onions, coarsely chopped
2 gloves garlic, crushed
½ cup parsley, chopped
½ cup butter
2 pounds beef chuck, coarsely chopped
1 pound pork shoulder, coarsely chopped
⅓ cup Gebhardt's brand chili powder
1 tablespoon salt
1½ teaspoon black pepper
1½ teaspoon ground cumin

Pick over and rinse the beans, then place in a Dutch oven with water to cover. Boil 2 minutes. Remove from heat, cover, and let stand 1 hour. Drain off liquid.

Rinse beans again. Add enough fresh water to cover. Bring to a boil. Reduce heat and simmer, covered, for 1 hour or until tender.

Stir in tomatoes and juice. Simmer 5 minutes. In a large skillet, sauté pepper in oil for 5 minutes. Add onion and cook until tender, stirring frequently. Stir in garlic and parsley. Add to the bean mixture. Use the same skillet to melt butter and sauté beef and pork until browned. Drain, then add to bean mixture along with chili powder, salt, pepper, and cumin.

Bring entire mixture to a boil, then reduce heat. Simmer covered for 1 hour. Uncover and cook 30 minutes more. Chili shouldn't be too thick. Skim off any excess fat and serve. Yields 6 hearty servings.

Chillin' Chilean Sea Bass and Spinach Salad

Chilean sea bass is the "hot" fish being served in all the trendy restaurants. It is delicious, especially when simply prepared and accompanied by something equally pure, such as this warm spinach salad. This will serve 8.

> **8 6-ounce sea bass fillets**
> **Sea salt and ground black pepper, to taste**
> **½ cup oil**
> **2 large bunches of spinach, washed and trimmed**
> **2 red onions, sliced**
> **4 cups mushrooms, sliced**
> **2 tomatoes, sliced**
> **½ pound bacon, cooked crisp and crumbled**
> **6 tablespoons sesame seeds**
> **2 tablespoons red wine vinegar**

Coat the fish with plenty of salt and pepper. Over medium heat, pour a few tablespoons of the oil in a large skillet. As soon as it begins to smoke, place the fillets into the skillet, skin down, until you notice the skin becoming crispy (approximately 5 to 7 minutes).

Using a spatula, turn the fish over and cook for another 5 to 7 minutes.

After thoroughly washing spinich, place the wet leaves in a covered saucepan with a tablespoon of water. Cook for 3 to 4 minutes on medium heat. The spinach should retain its bright color and shape. Keep warm on the side until recipe is completed.

Quickly pour the rest of your oil into the pan with the fish, increasing the heat to medium-high, then add onions, mushrooms, tomatoes, bacon, and sesame seeds. Toss for 1 minute, then add the vinegar and give it a rapid stir. Add salt and pepper to taste.

Serve the mouth-watering fish atop the steamed spinach. They make the ideal couple!

Offbeat BBQ Kebabs

Usually, grilling outside can be such an ordeal that I keep it simple . . . burgers, chicken breasts, fish, and veggie kebabs. This is an interesting recipe I've experimented with for "Liula" kebabs. It's more work, but a nice change from the standard fare. Besides, think how cute you'll look in your "Kiss the Cook" apron.

4 pounds lean ground lamb
12 tablespoons fresh mint leaves
4 teaspoons salt
½ cup onions, chopped
12 scallions, chopped
1 tablespoon ground black pepper
2 tablespoons garlic, minced
½ tablespoon ginger powder
1 tablespoon red pepper flakes
Shot of Tabasco

While the coals are heating, mix the lamb in a large bowl with all your ingredients. Form this concoction into eight sausages, approximately 3 inches by 2 inches.

Soak wooden skewers in water for at least 10 minutes, then thread sausages onto them. You can skewer on some veggies, too, if you like . . . baby tomatoes, onions, bell peppers.

Grill over the coals for about 15 minutes or until thoroughly cooked. Very tasty.

Serve with pita bread and hummus.

Fun food fact: Rotisserie is not just a meat-cooking method! The Merriam-Webster Dictionary defines rotisserie *as an adjective meaning of, relating to, or being a sports league consisting of imaginary teams whose performance is based on the statistics of actual players. Imaginary sports!? That's my kind of athleticism!*

Versatile Wine Marinade for Groovy Grilling

While we're on the subject of grilling, here's an easy, adaptable recipe for a marinade, which will add flavor, color, and texture to your meat of choice. Opt for red wine when making beef or lamb, white wine for fish or poultry. Just whisk all the ingredients together into a large, non-reactive bowl, which you may then use for marinating, turning the food at least once an hour to ensure complete coverage. Or, you may prefer to marinate in sealable plastic bags, which keep the food thoroughly covered with the mixture.

1 bottle of red or white wine
½ cup olive oil
1 onion, minced
1 garlic clove, minced
2 tablespoons fresh Italian parsley
2 tablespoons of your desired spice, preferably fresh (tarragon, sage, rosemary, thyme, dill, etc.), chopped
1 teaspoon salt
1 teaspoon red pepper flakes

Soul-Sister's Sole Meuniere

A classic dish, ideal for time-crunched chefs and lighter dining. So simple! Don't use frozen fish, however, as fresh fillets are the only choice for this one. And don't trust the Gorton's Fisherman, even if you like that older, salty type. (Remember when Denny Moore was young, hunky "Tongo" on *Gilligan's Island*? No wonder that, with "Ginger's" glamour competing with "Mary Ann's" culinary prowess under the most dire circumstances, he couldn't possibly make a choice between them. We're lucky . . . we can strive to possess the attributes of both ladies!)

1 fresh sole fillet per person
Sea salt and ground black pepper, to taste
Flour for dredging
1 tablespoon unsalted butter per serving
1 tablespoon olive oil per serving
Sliced, seeded lemon (½ lemon per serving)
Sea salt and black pepper, to taste
Fresh cilantro, chopped

Lightly season the fillets with salt and pepper, then cover completely in flour, patting them gently as a baby to ensure coverage.

Heat butter and oil in a large skillet on medium heat, using approximately 1 tbsp. of butter and 1 tbsp. of oil for each fillet you are preparing. Once it is all dissolved and mixed, shake off excess flour from fillets and place them in the skillet.

In about 5 minutes, the fish will turn golden, indicating that it is cooked. Turn and brown the other side.

Remove fish from skillet. To make the sauce, add lemon slices to the butter/oil mixture, adding butter if needed. Stir on low heat and sprinkle in more salt, pepper, and chopped cilantro. This sauce can now top the fillets, which you will serve immediately with a frigid glass of crisp Pinot Grigio! Here's to Sherwood Schwartz!

Dinner's over. Do you know what to do with your utensils? Place knife and fork together, side by side, on the plate. The knife blade faces inward and the fork is upside down so that the tines touch the plate. Get your elbows off the table! The end of the main course doesn't designate the decline of modern civilization!

DESSERTS

Everyone's going to be full after the main course, so don't hurry the final act of your culinary extravaganza—let 'em have a breather. You don't, however, want them to wander off back to the living room or outside for a smoke. You've got to keep the momentum going. Quickly get the table cleared and cleaned of all main course remnants so that everyone is comfortable staying put. In her nineteenth-century cookbook, *Everyday Cookery*, the sage Isabella Beaton advised, "Clear as you go. Muddle makes more muddle."

"After a good dinner one can forgive anybody, even one's own relations." —OSCAR WILDE (1854–1900)

I always make a pot of strong, decaffeinated coffee (no flavored coffee to interfere with your gastronomic creations). Even if no one opts for a cup, the aroma will go from the nostrils directly to the brain to say: dessert's coming!

Like directing a script, this is a great time to segue the conversation into a lighter tone. If you enjoy playing after-dinner games like Charades or Mystery Date, this is where the groundwork is laid. Or even if you just plan to sit around and gab the rest of the night away (which is almost always the case *chez moi*), it should be jovial and gay from here on in. Take a theme from the dinner conversation and make a light observation about it. This will keep folks talking until they're ready to savor your dessert creation.

If the main course was heavy, go light on the dessert. If not, go for broke. I'm generally health and weight conscious in my menu planning, but this is when it's okay to break some rules. Remember, every day is someone's birthday, so celebrate!

Serving cake? Check the Internet for celebrities born on the date of your party and honor them! Your guests will get a kick out of singing Happy Birthday *to Elvis, Ed Asner, or Emperor Hirohito!*

Don't be offended if someone refuses dessert. They may be full, or operating on some secret diet regimen. Being easy-going is the true art to hosting, and that goes for everything from a guest who shows up in cut-off shorts to everyone bemoaning your intentions to play Truth or Dare. Games and themes are wonderful ways to promote conversations, but should not be used to *replace* them.

After the dessert course is the only time in the evening you can get away with not clearing away the dishes. Of course, you'll have to if you're going to remain gathered around the table chatting or playing cards. But if you drift back toward the living or family rooms with aperitifs, it's perfectly all right to let the table remain temporarily unattended. That is, at least until you're alone or have a discreet moment to load up the dishwasher. (It also might come in handy to clear a plate or two when trying to signal the evening's end. See "Saying Good Night.")

Wondering what to do with that napkin when the meal is over? Place it loosely next to the plate, approximately where it was located when you first sat down. In spite of Emily Post, I say it's okay to fold it neatly in half. It is only permitted to leave the napkin on your seat if you have to excuse yourself from the table during dinner. Never put it on your empty plate.

Even if you're on a diet, go ahead and indulge in a small portion, too. You wind up making guests feel guilty if they're eating and you're not. Some ripe, washed fruit in a prominently displayed bowl can always be used for a compromise if any caloric dispute erupts.

A side note on dieting, in case you care. I've tried every plan known to man and can swear on my Niagara Falls spoon rest that the only diet that *really* works is *portion control.* Joan Crawford once told a reporter that her secret to a slim figure was miniscule servings at mealtime. "I'm the hungriest woman in Hollywood!" she claimed. Just do me a favor and don't exercise that kind of manic discipline when you're sitting at *my* table!

"As long as you're going to think anyway, you might as well think Big!"
*—*DONALD TRUMP

Fat-Free Brownies with Hot Orange-Raspberry Sauce

I invented this one while on the Weight Watchers program. You're not only going fat free, but serving small portions of this rich treat will cut down on the calories, too. Make the brownies before the party and the sauce can be prepared within 3 minutes of serving. Fortunately, with treats that are this tasty, you won't have to *fudge* to your friends; my gal pal Nancy still hasn't forgiven me for the faux "Fat-Free Five Cheese Pizza" incident. I can't recall how many slices she tucked away before I had to confess my carb-spiracy!

¾ cup unsweetened apple butter
1 cup sugar
1 cup brown sugar
2 teaspoons vanilla extract
1 cup egg substitute
¾ cup cocoa powder
1 cup flour
½ teaspoon baking powder
Nonstick cooking spray
1½ cup canned raspberry pie filling
⅓ cup fresh orange juice
Frozen or fresh raspberries for garnish

Preheat oven to 350 degrees. In a large bowl, combine apple butter, sugars, vanilla, and egg substitute. Mix until blended. In a separate bowl, mix cocoa, flour, and baking powder. Add to larger bowl and mix both together.

Spray baking dish with cooking spray and spoon in batter. Bake for 30 to 35 minutes.

The sauce is a mixture of 1½ cups of raspberry pie filling, heated in a saucepan with ⅓ cup of orange juice. Bring the mixture to a boil, then drizzle it over the cooled brownies. Sprinkle fresh berries atop the dessert and around the plates.

If you like fat-free whipped cream, put a dollop on the brownie before adding the sauce. If Sarah "Fergie" Ferguson is on your guest list, limit her to *one* portion!

Fat-tastic Fudge

If your main course is gargantuan, fudge is a good dessert option—just a taste of chocolate to satisfy the sweet tooth. If there's any left over, sprinkle with a little powdered sugar and wrap it up in some aluminum foil with a ribbon tied around it. Send it home with your guests and wish them "sweet dreams." This is also great for setting out on pretty plates while playing after-dinner games or sipping Frangelico or Sambuca. (If serving the latter, toss 3 coffee beans into each glass as a wish for good luck. But don't try to be continental and light your drink. It's not only a fire hazard in your hands, you'll burn off all the alcohol!

1½ cups granulated sugar
⅔ cup evaporated milk
1 tablespoon butter
¼ teaspoon salt
2 cups mini-marshmallows
1½ cups chocolate morsels
½ cup chopped walnuts
1 teaspoon vanilla extract
1½ cups chocolate morsels
Nonstick cooking spray

In a saucepan, combine the sugar, milk, butter, and salt over medium heat. Stir and cook for 5 minutes at a rolling boil.

Remove from heat and stir in your mini-marshmallows, chocolate morsels, walnuts, and vanilla. Give this a good stir until the marshmallows completely melt, then pour the mixture into a baking pan sprayed with non-stick spray. Stick it in the fridge for at least 2 to 3 hours, then cut and serve.

"A woman who does a good job in the kitchen is sure to reap her rewards in other rooms!" —BETTY WHITE (as the horny homemaker "Sue Ann Nivens," *The Mary Tyler Moore Show*)

Hollywood Cheesecake of the Rich and Famous

My fit friends, personal trainers Nancy Kennedy and Bobby Strom, regularly work with big stars like Britney Spears, Julia Roberts, Kevin Costner and Jennifer Lopez, not only putting them through their paces in the gym, but also acting as "Fridge Doctors." They rummage through the refrigerator and perform a complete makeover on all the food and beverages found inside. Ha! That's why they're my only two buddies who have never been invited over to my place. My medicine chest could survive anyone's scrutiny and I defy anyone to conduct a white-glove test even on top of the ceiling fans, but nutritionists in my icebox?! No way!

Their suggestion for coping with the lure of decadent desserts is not to deny oneself, but rather to share servings. They do, however, have a tasty low-fat cheesecake recipe that you can hoard all to yourself! (But do keep in mind, it serves 10!) It contains only 94.7 calories and 1.21 grams of fat per serving. With numbers like that, you won't even feel guilty if you sneak a leftover piece out of the fridge in the middle of the night.

3 packages fat-free cream cheese, softened
¾ cup sugar substitute, such as Splenda
1 teaspoon vanilla extract
4 egg whites
Nonstick cooking spray
⅓ cup graham cracker crumbs
1½ cups strawberries, sliced

Preheat oven to 325 degrees.

With an electric mixer, combine the cream cheese, sugar substitute, and vanilla in a bowl until well blended. Add egg whites and blend into cream cheese mixture, careful not to overmix.

Spray a 9-inch pie plate with the cooking spray. Add some spray to the graham cracker crumbs to moisten and mix them together. Pack the crumbs into the bottom and sides of the pie plate, and then pour in the cream cheese mixture.

Bake for 45 minutes or until center has almost set. Remove from the oven and let cool, then refrigerate for at least three hours. Top with strawberries and serve.

Oatmeal Raisin d'Etre Cookies

Pardon the *franglais*, but these tasty treats might just be the meaning of life. Fun to eat any time of the year (or any time of the day!), but especially comforting around the Yuletide ... when it sometimes dips below 70 here in Hollywood.

If for some unimaginable reason you have any left over, or if they start to go stale, crumble them over vanilla yogurt for a snack.

1¼ cups all purpose flour
1 teaspoon baking soda
1 teaspoon ground cinnamon powder
½ teaspoon salt
2 sticks of butter, softened
¾ cup granulated sugar
¾ cup brown sugar
1 teaspoon vanilla extract
2 eggs
3 cups quick oats
1 cup chopped walnuts
1⅓ cups raisins

Preheat oven to 375 degrees. In a bowl, mix together the flour, baking soda, cinnamon, and salt. Using a mixer, add the butter, white and brown sugars, and vanilla and beat until smooth. Next, beat in the eggs one at a time. Finish by stirring in the oats, nuts, and raisins.

Put rounded pieces of the dough onto ungreased cookie sheets. I'm often tempted to make them too big. But don't! Think a little bigger than tablespoon-size.

Bake at 375 degrees for 8 to 9 minutes. Exercise a little discipline and let them cool on the sheets for 5 minutes before you attack them. This will yield more than 3 dozen cookies.

Morning Maven's Potent Pudding

For over a decade, lovely Lorraine Kelly (that's her on page 101) has been the United Kingdom's reigning Queen of Morning "Breakfast" Television. I started working with her via satellite in 2002 and it's easy to see why her millions of fans are so captivated and ferociously loyal. When the sultry Scotswoman isn't dazzling viewers in front of the cameras, she's a domestic dream, whipping up creations like "Cranachan," a traditional pudding dish. This is her version "with a wee Scottish surprise." Not the kind you'd find under Mel Gibson's kilt, but a smile-inducer, nonetheless!

1 ounce rolled oats
1 pint double cream
3 tablespoons honey
Very generous shot of a good Scottish malt whiskey*
4 tablespoons natural yogurt
6 ounces fresh raspberries

Toast the oats under the grill until golden brown, then allow to cool. Whip the cream, honey, and whiskey together until it softens. Fold in the yogurt.

Spoon the mixture into a serving dish and chill for a few hours. To serve, sprinkle the oatmeal over the mixture and place the raspberries in the center.

Lorraine says, "It is very sweet, but yummy. Have lots of whiskey on hand to toast each other as you guzzle the pudding! Alternately, just quaff the whiskey and forget all about cooking anything!"

Cheers, sweetie!

Blue-Ribbon Pecan Pie

No lie, this one took home the blue ribbon at my Neighborhood Harvest Festival's Annual Bake-Off, trouncing ultra-stiff competition from *thirtysomething*'s Melanie Mayron and Oscar winner Linda Hunt. The secret ingredient: the chocolate! *Extra* correspondent Michael Corbett, head of the Block Committee, didn't bake anything, but he did designate me in charge of all new trees planted on our block. Too bad they couldn't afford my favorite, the Aspen (natch)!

Before it comes out in the tabloids, I will admit that I used a store-bought, whole wheat pie crust because there are simply some

*Lorraine recommends Highland Park brand whiskey. "My favorite from the Orkney Islands in the north of Scotland. It is our most northerly distillery and the whiskey has a very smooth taste." Maybe that's where "Merry, Queen of Scots" came from! Lorraine suggests using a "dram," which measures to ⅛ ounce, but that's not generous enough for a true Scotsman, so follow your instincts when pouring!

things I cannot master. I suggest you do the same, or call your mother for her crust recipe. That said, I will continue.

3 eggs
½ cup dark corn syrup
½ cup dark brown sugar
4 tablespoons butter, melted
1 teaspoon vanilla extract
½ cup molasses
½ cup chocolate chips, melted
Your Mother's Pie Crust, or store-bought pre-made
½ cup pecans, chopped
¾ cup pecan halves
chocolate covered espresso beans (optional)

Preheat oven to 425 degrees. Beat the eggs in a bowl until the yolks and whites are blended. Add the corn syrup, brown sugar, melted butter, vanilla, molasses, and chocolate chips and blend well.

Put the pie shell or rolled out dough into the pie dish and sprinkle with the chopped pecans.

Stir the pecan halves into the syrup mixture and pour into the pie shell.

Bake 15 minutes, then reduce heat to 350 degrees and continue baking for another 15 to 20 minutes, just until the edges are set. You'll notice a provocative little quiver from the center of the pie, telling you to remove it from the oven.

While the pie is still hot, place the espresso beans on top. Design a pattern you think will win you the competition!

Put on the Pounds Cake

Growing up, every birthday in our household was marked with a traditional pound cake. "Pound of sugar, pound of flour, pound of butter," Mom used to say was the recipe. It's not quite that evil, but close. It's also sublime when topped with berries, whipped cream, gelato, you name it.

If you happen to be having overnight guests (planned or unplanned, heh heh heh!), this is spectacular to wake up to with a cup of hot coffee.

3 cups sugar
1 cup shortening
½ pound butter
1 teaspoon salt
8 eggs
1 cup whole milk
4 teaspoons vanilla
4 cups flour
4 teaspoons baking powder

Preheat oven to 350 degrees. Beat all ingredients in one bowl until smooth. Grease and flour one large baking pan and one smaller pan. Pour ¾ of the mixture into the larger pan and the remainder in the smaller. Bake 1 hour. The cake will rise and expand, turning a gorgeous golden brown. A toothpick won't be long enough, so use a wooden skewer to test . . . Insert and it should come out clean. Simple and sinful—diets be damned!

Mrs. D's Ginger Creams

As a fat high school'er (tipping the scale at a max of nearly 200 pounds!), I was the team mascot, not a player (go, Eagles!). The valedictorian, not the prom king. I *was* the student body in the grossest sense of the term. So while my classmates were attending keg parties and sporting hickies, I was over at Mrs. DeHart's house baking (and *eating*) these delicious cookies. They're traditional Yuletide fare, but don't wait till then to try them. This makes about 3 dozen, or in my adolescent case, one good snack!!

¼ cup shortening
½ cup sugar
1 egg
⅓ cup molasses
2 cups sifted flour
½ teaspoon baking soda
½ teaspoon salt
1 teaspoon ginger
½ teaspoon cinnamon
½ teaspoon cloves
½ cup water

Preheat oven to 400 degrees. Cream together shortening and sugar, then beat in an egg. Gradually stir in molasses. Sift in a third of the dried ingredients, then pour in a third of your water. Repeat this step twice and all your ingredients will be combined.

Drop the mixture by teaspoons, approximately 2 inches apart, onto a greased cookie sheet. Bake at 400 degrees, 8 to 10 minutes. Frost while warm.

Butter Cream Frosting:

⅓ cup butter
1 teaspoon vanilla
2 cups sifted confectioner's sugar
2 tablespoons evaporated milk

Cream butter. Add vanilla, then gradually add sugar. Finally, add evaporated milk and beat until smooth.

Incidentally, Mrs. D is still a great, supportive friend, even after all these years have passed and all those pounds have been shed! Hee hee . . . I just cannot wait for the 25th reunion!

Kaya's Ultimate Temptation: Caramel Apple Pie

When the reality TV trend began to sweep the airwaves, hunky Kaya Wittenburg was one of its first major sensations, appearing on the memorable Fox offering *Temptation Island*. As the brawny bachelor with the teddy bear–like devotion to his girlfriend, Valerie, he captured the hearts of millions of viewers and has since capitalized on his "sweet n' sexy" persona by writing a book, pursuing his modeling career, and making scads of personal appearances. I've even used him on a few of my TV reports whenever a playful playboy is called for. He's obliged my cameras with stories on men's nipple waxing, kiddy costume parties, dressing to disguise figure faults (if he has any, they are *very* well hidden) and even chocolate body paints. His natural charm and charisma . . . oh, yeah, and his *pecs* . . . make even the most absurd situations seem fun and foxy! Lucky Valerie!

And, amazingly, he cooks, too! This one is direct from his kitchen and he tells me, "This is my favorite dessert. I can't resist it! I really like to gob on the caramel and serve a la mode with vanilla ice cream." Feeling tempted, anyone??

2¼ cups all-purpose flour
2½ cups butter

6 tablespoons whole milk
1 cup sugar
1 teaspoon ground cinnamon
6 cups Jonathan apples, chopped
½ cup caramel apple dip mix (liquid in a jar)
½ cup brown sugar, packed

Preheat oven to 350 degrees.

To prepare the pie crust, use a pastry blender and cut 2 cups cold butter into 1 cup of flour until pieces are pea-sized. Sprinkle 1 tablespoon of milk over part of the mixture, then toss with a fork. Repeat 3 more times, using 1 tablespoon of milk each time, until all the dough is moistened. Shape into a ball. Then, on a lightly floured surface, roll it from the center to edges in a 12-inch circle.

Wrap pastry around a rolling pin, then unroll into a 9-inch pie tin. Trim to just beyond the edges of the tin, then carefully crimp.

To make the filling, in a large bowl mix sugar, another ¼ cup of flour and cinnamon. Add the apples and toss until coated. Place in pie crust.

Combine 2 tablespoons of the caramel apple dip and 2 tablespoons of milk, then drizzle over apple mixture. Reserve some of the caramel for topping.

In a mixing bowl, combine another cup of flour and brown sugar. Cut in ½ cup cold butter till mixture resembles coarse crumbs. Sprinkle over filling and cover the outer edge of pie crust with aluminum foil to prevent over-browning. Place on baking sheet.

Bake for 30 minutes. Remove foil, then bake another 25 to 30 minutes until golden brown. Cool for 10 minutes before drizzling the remaining caramel dip over the top. Cool pie on wire rack.

This is crumbly and delicious, with the wonderful caramel-apple combination of flavors that will take you back to your childhood . . . or, better yet, to your own Temptation Island!

Mom Mom's Chocolate Cake

My little old grandmother in Pennsylvania still makes one of these babies for anyone in her neighborhood who is having a birthday. I always make sure to time my visits around someone's party so I can have my annual ingestion of Crisco. Once she did manage to get her hand caught in the mixer, so proceed with caution when folding ingredients! Mom Mom's still going strong as she nears her centennial . . . in fact, at her most recent physical, the doctor advised her to get new boxing gloves! No matter how many times she gets knocked down, she keeps getting back up (must be that good German stock). She also continues to lead the cheering section from the bleachers at her high school's annual Thanksgiving Day football games and even caught the ball one year. She's a local institution! Lots of teenaged tight ends have been titillated by this recipe over the years . . . and you'll love it, too; the coffee makes it incredibly dark and moist. Recipes don't get more tried and true than this one. For added decadence, grease the cake pan with real butter.

2 cups sugar
2 cups flour
½ cup shortening
¾ cup unsweetened cocoa
1 teaspoon vanilla
2 teaspoons baking soda
¼ teaspoon salt
2 eggs
1 teaspoon baking powder
1 cup whole milk
¼ cup hot coffee

Preheat oven to 400.

Combine all ingredients and beat on high with a mixer 10 to 15 minutes until smooth.

Bake for 30 to 35 minutes.

Cake is finished when a toothpick inserted into the center comes out clean.

Chocolate Icing:

1 pound (!) powdered sugar
1 tablespoon butter
1 teaspoon vanilla
6 to 8 teaspoons cocoa
Whole milk, as needed

Mix ingredients, adding whole milk until the icing has a smooth consistency.

Wait for cake to cool before icing.

> *"Getting old . . . it's not nice, but it's interesting."*
> —AUGUST STRINDBERG (1849–1912)

Gram's Icebox Cake

As talented as my Mom Mom is at baking from scratch, my other grandmother, Gram, was definitely culinary challenged. (She wasn't lacking in the longevity department, though, cavorting with her nightly pitchers of Manhattans and incessant cigarette puffing until she was 99. Clad in her favorite pink running suit and Reeboks, she was an adorable firecracker!) You know you're in trouble when you're more excited by her handmade nylon netting potscrubbies than you are by her Saharan Pineapple Upside Down Cake. That's why most of her better recipes started out with cake mix, and my dad at eighty years of age, would still prefer a can of Spaghetti-O's over anything Julia Child could dream up.

This was one of Gram's tastier triumphs that every kid in the world will love to help construct and then later demolish with a fork . . . even after they're grown up and a member of AARP! The Icebox Cake is also great for summer since it requires no baking. For Gram, that fact greatly helped to reduce the risk of failure.

> 2 cups whipped cream (whip your own, or cheat like Gram did and
>   use frozen topping)
> 1 teaspoon vanilla
> 2 9-ounce packages of chocolate wafers (you'll have plenty left over,
>   but buy two boxes because they break so easily. They're thinner
>   than Lara Flynn Boyle!)
> Chocolate sprinkles or cocoa powder

Stir vanilla extract into whipped cream and spread onto individual wafers, approximately ½ tablespoon on each. Arrange these into a log by stacking the wafers. Stand more wafers on end at the edges and frost over the outside with remaining whipped cream.

Refrigerate several hours until the whipped cream becomes firm. Remove 15 to 30 minutes before serving and decorate with cocoa powder or jimmies (the Philadelphia vernacular for "sprinkles").

When serving, cut slices of the log at an angle to keep it from crumbling. And if it falls apart, so what?! It tastes just as good!

Mrs. California's Peanut Butter Pageant Bars

I was honored to be a judge at the 2003 Mrs. California International Pageant in Anaheim, California. As cheesy as those kinds of competitions may be, this was a truly touching experience . . . to meet these women and their husbands, who were vying for the crown based on their dedication and service to both family and their respective California communities. Of course, being sequestered at Disneyland with some other fun judges wasn't all bad, either, especially when one judge was Laurie Coleman, the hotter-than-hot wife of Minnesota Senator Norman Coleman (she is the lady who can show you the real meaning of the word *hootenanny!*) and the equally hot heir (not to be confused with "hot air"), pro snowboarder/vintner Carlo Mondavi. It was a pretty wild weekend, especially when two ABC soap hunks nearly came to blows over the same woman. The older one was a married dad and, by the end of the night, had a little person nestled in his lap. And I mean *little person* in the politically correct terminology . . . she wasn't merely diminutive. Family values are obviously not as important to him in his real life as to his patriarchal Pine Valley character. Ohh, it was all so very, very weird . . .

> *"I have a life," a fan at the ABC Super Soap Weekend enthusiastically defended, while sipping Cosmopolitans. "I just prefer to live it in Pine Valley."*

The 2003 title winner was the lovely and charismatic contestant from Sacramento, Chyrissee (pronounced "Sha-reese") Lee, and I asked her—as the first official act of her new reign—to contribute her favorite recipe. She gave me this one and praised it for its minimal ingredients and easy preparation. She calls them "Reese Cookies," which I assume is not only a play on her name but also an homage to the famous peanut butter and chocolate candies even E.T. loved to eat.

¼ cup butter or margarine, softened
1 pound powdered sugar
1 8-ounce jar peanut butter
2¼ cups graham crackers, crushed in blender
2 8-ounce milk chocolate bars

Mix together margarine, sugar, peanut butter, and crushed crackers, then press evenly into 9 x 13 glass pan. In the microwave, melt chocolate bars and spread over mixture.

Chill in refrigerator for at least 2 hours until candy is set. Cut at room temperature. Makes 24 bars.

Incidentally, the Mrs. California International was not my first exposure to the world of pageants. I co-wrote and produced the first-ever Mr. Romance Cover Model Pageant, in which dozens of long haired he-men contended to unseat Fabio for a lucrative stint adorning the fronts of paperback bodice-rippers. Fabio was amazingly gracious and a good sport throughout the madness, and judge Cesar Romero was even more debonair and charming than his "Joker" counterpart! You can't even begin to imagine the audience of screaming ladies. I'll stick with the "Mrs." . . . thanks, very much!

Carol Connors' Gold Record Carat Cake

My punny-pal, Academy Award–nominated songwriter Carol Connors, has had her share of gold records. As a member of the Teddy Bears, she crooned "To Know, Know, Know Him . . . is to Love, Love, Love Him" and she's known, known, known in motion picture circles for her work on the *Rocky* theme and *The Pianist*. But she can also make music in the kitchen! This recipe won her a cook-off at the famed L.A. eatery *Le Dome* and she even had it presented by some curvy Playboy Bunnies, which prompted Hugh

Hefner to quip that her first place prize had as much to do with presentation as it did with the cake, itself! Try it out and brainstorm your own happy ending.

- **2 cups sugar**
- **2 cups flour**
- **2 teaspoons baking powder**
- **2 teaspoons baking soda**
- **½ teaspoon salt**
- **4 eggs**
- **1 cup oil**
- **3 cups finely grated raw carrots**
- **¼ cup nuts**
- **Additional raisins, coconut, or pineapple, optional**

Preheat oven to 350 degrees. Mix the sugar, flour, baking powder, baking soda, salt, eggs, and oil by hand. Do not use a mixer. Then add the rest of the ingredients and mix well. Bake in a greased 9x13 pan for one hour at 350 degrees.

Carol's Creamy Dreamy Frosting:

- **4 ounces cream cheese**
- **¼ cup butter**
- **1¾ cups powdered sugar**
- **1 teaspoon vanilla**
- **Your choice of raisins, coconut, or pineapple here, too!**

Soften cream cheese and butter to room temperature, and beat together in a small bowl. Add sugar and vanilla, and continue until well blended. If needed, add a little milk to make into a smooth, spreadable consistency. If you decide to add raisins, coconut, or pineapple, do that last, and use a spoon to combine.

While baking, Carol came up with these lyrics to sing to the tune of *Diamonds Are a Girl's Best Friend.*

A spinach soufflé may be so continental,
But carats are a girl's best friend.
A rhubarb surprise may hide more than it's meant to,
But carats are a girl's best friend.
Carats cooked . . . or carats sliced,
Carats raw . . . or carats delight.
So wear it, or bare it,
Please pass me the carat!
Carats are a girl's best friend!

BEVERAGES

Variety is the spice of life. The most important beverage choice you can make is to offer an assortment of non-alcoholic drinks for anyone who can't/won't touch the hard stuff. If someone has overdone it on the liquor, you are responsible to cut 'em off and sober 'em up. Since this is not always easy or within your specific control, don't hesitate to call a cab or make up the guest room or futon. Most cab companies give out refrigerator magnets with their numbers, which are useful to have for such situations.

Glenn's Aunt Jeannie's advice on mixing the perfect Screwdriver: When it comes to the ratio of vodka to orange juice: "It's no good unless you can see through it!" God bless her, Aunt Jeannie wasn't around very long. . . .

Good red and/or white table wines are *de rigeur*, and I'm not a slave to any certain vintages, although Coppolla's Bianco is always on ice for when 5 o'clock finally rolls around! Serve what you like and what you know others enjoy. If your guests have brought bottles, pour them a glass of yours first, and make a special fuss over opening theirs at the dinner table. If it's something you know to be horrible, feign delight in saving it for some future *cause celebre*.

Stuck for an idea when a friend or family member asks what you'd like to receive for your birthday/anniversary/Hanukah? Why not request membership in a wine club? Never is that hunky UPS man more welcome to appear on the threshold than when he's laying a case of wine at your feet!

For *al fresco* dining, homemade wine coolers, sangria, and margaritas are fun to make and drink. I'm lucky enough to have a prolific lemon tree in my backyard, and it's always fun to ask a guest to go out and pick some to slice for garnishing the glasses.

Wine charms are inexpensive, pretty *accoutrements* to adorn your stemware and help guests avoid mixing up their drinks with someone else's. They're increasingly popular in most home or kitchen departments, and each wraps right around the stem to personalize and identify each glass. Eeeww, you don't want to accidentally sip after Cold-Sore Cassie, do you!?

A pitcher of cold, fresh water is an essential part of your table setting. Many people won't think or want to ask for it unless it's offered, and water is needed not just to keep alcohol consumption at a sane pace, but for cleansing the palate, too.

Beautify a plain glass pitcher of water with colorful, edible items frozen inside ice cubes. Mint leaves, citrus slices, violets, and berries are all good ideas.

Killer Bloody Marys

When coping with the assorted triumphs and tragedies that come with nearly a half-century of matrimony, one of my parents' saving graces is a macabre sense of humor. At their house, BEWARE OF SNAKES signs help keep trespassers off the front lawn . . . misdirected vultures are now seasonal guests courtesy of my folks' encouragement and a few tasty live mice . . . careful what drawer you open: There may be a severed (rubber) hand waiting for you. When my dad was a practicing orthopedic surgeon, there were always lots of gory medical mags lying around so I, too, developed a penchant for the *Grand Guignol*. I've always mused that our clan is a cross between the Addams family and the Carringtons. Maybe that's why my parents nicknamed one of their particularly rambunctious great-grandkids "666"!

Named for the murderous monarch Mary Tudor (daughter of Henry VIII and granddaughter to Christopher Columbus' patrons Ferdinand and Isabella of Spain), these potent potables are especially significant for our clan. Queen Mary actually sentenced our ancestor, Archbishop Thomas Cranmer, to die a fiery death for heresy (he was a Protestant). We often toast to his memory and bravery in the face of a death especially torturous, in that his execution was carried out on a rainy day and the fire kept getting doused.

Here is a delicious guide to preparing bone-chilling Bloody Marys, which my parents like to serve while clad all in black. They once had their local mortician over to pre-plan their final arrangements and toasted him with tumblers of this thick thirst quencher. He was not amused, but after a glass or two, even he managed to warm up to their cold-blooded comedy!

1 pitcher tomato juice (don't use the salt-free)
Worcestershire sauce, to taste
Bermuda sherry peppers or Tabasco, to taste
1 whole lemon
1 teaspoon horseradish
Celery salt and pepper, to taste
Horseradish
Large green olives (pitted) or jalapeño peppers
Celery stalks for garnish
Top-shelf vodka

The spooky secret to this is to be creative with the measurements. If you have a spicy crowd, go for lots of heat! And make sure to serve these drinks in big glasses with crisp, fresh celery stalks for garnish. Since teetotalers won't want the alcohol (or maybe someone will want theirs made "light"), we Aspens create the mix in a pitcher and then add the vodka individually to each glass we pour.

Fill the pitcher with tomato juice (V-8 is yummy, too), then add dashes of Worcestershire, Tabasco, or Outerbridge's Sherry Peppers if you remembered to pick up a bottle the last time you were in Bermuda. Squeeze in the juice of one whole lemon (any pulp is okay, as well) and a big tablespoon of prepared horseradish. Add celery salt and pepper to taste, and garnish each glass with a celery stalk.

It's fun to make these "chunky" by adding either mild jalapeño peppers or green olives. I've also seen pickled string beans substituted for the celery stalks. Kosher salt on the rim of the glasses is fun for extra effect.

The wonderful *melange* of flavors goes down so deliciously you won't want to make them too strong with the liquor. Then you might really have a scary scene on your hands!

Desert Martinis

Ahh, the sixties! Mother and Dad used to mix up a pitcher of these every night before dinner. They named this complicated concoction for the desert because it is oh-so dry. These days, martini-wannabes include ingredients ranging from flavored vodkas to chocolate liqueurs, but *this* is the original, baby!

1 bottle of Beefeater's, Bombay, Boodles, or other top-shelf gin

Keep the gin in the freezer for a few hours. Or in Mother and Dad's case, it just happens to reside there. Once very cold, pour gin into a martini pitcher containing a few ice cubes. Allow an unopened bottle of vermouth to observe from a discreet distance. Twenty-nine is the lucky number of stirs you make in a clockwise motion before straining off the ice and pouring into elegant martini glasses. Two plump, green olives speared and placed inside your beverage will highlight this delicious cocktail.

One should never partake in more than a *single* martini (especially these Desert Martinis, which are virtually *sans* dilution!). It is gauche and could be dangerous to the future course of the evening's events. All of a sudden, you toast, "Bottoms Up!" and someone obliges . . . literally!

Savory Sangria

1 pineapple
2 oranges
2 bottles dry red wine, such as Coppola's mellow, fruity *Rosso*
2 tablespoons sugar
2 ounces Triple Sec
2 quarts club soda

Slice the fruit thinly, combine with wine, sugar, and Triple Sec. Refrigerate for at least 4 hours.

Just before serving, mix with club soda and garnish with orange peel. I like to use clay pitchers. Put ice in the pitchers, but not in the glasses into which the sangria is poured.

Marita's Margaritas

Making and serving this Mexican mixer is already festive enough, but when one of your best friends is margarita-drinking Marita, you have to re-christen it! She opened her own jazz bar in the French Quarter of New Orleans a few years ago and makes a special version of the classic cocktail you will certainly savor sipping. (Incidentally, I once shared a pitcher with the delightful Heather Locklear . . . she is as fun loving and adorable as you'd like to think she is and extremely good natured with her ardent *female* admirers! I often wonder if she still has the caricature I drew of us all at the little Tex Mex place on that sun-soaked and tequila drenched Sunday afternoon.)

1 bottle top-shelf tequila
1 bottle Triple Sec
Limes for juicing, to taste
Splash of orange juice
Splash of 7 Up
Salt
Ice

Don't use anything but wonderful tequila or your *cabesa* will be throbbing the next morning. I make these by the pitcher, almost always served on the rocks, but you can blend them if you desire.

Combine 3 parts tequila, to 1 part Triple Sec. Squeeze in lime juice to taste and shake or stir until blended. Splash in the OJ and 7 Up, then serve with lots of ice in a salt-rimmed glass garnished with a lime wedge.

Sorry not to be more exact with the measurements for this one, but half the fun is being reckless with the pouring! For added drama, float some citrus peel in the center of each glass, pour in some alcohol, and light it for a Flaming Fiesta! And the next time you're in the Big Easy, be sure to stop in to Johnny White's Sports Bar and say hi to Marita!

Tangerine Lemonade, Honey!
(The Punch That Doesn't Pack One!)

Every fall, I harvest scores of fresh tangerines right in the backyard. So Cal living is *so* wonderful! If they're not in season where you live, use any warm-colored, sweet-tasting citrus, like pink grapefruit. Yield: 12 big cups.

8 large tangerines
2 lemons
1 cup honey
7 cups water
2 cups mixed berries
Mint sprigs
Maraschino cherries (optional)

Squeeze the tangerines and lemons into a large pitcher, then gradually stir in honey until combined. Add the water and the mixed berries (I like bright red raspberries). After letting it chill for a few hours, serve in tall, frosted glasses half filled with crushed ice and garnish with mint sprigs.

If you want to expand this and make a festive punch, use half the recipe above (without the mixed berries) and freeze it in a decorative mold.

Slide it into a punch bowl filled with a mixture of 1 quart ginger ale and 1 cup pineapple juice. Float your mint sprigs and berries on top, or in a salute to Shirley Temple, toss in a maraschino cherry!

To chill your glasses, keep them in the refrigerator or filled with ice until ready to pour and serve the drinks. It's also pretty to run the bowls of your cocktail glass stemware under cold water, then place them in the freezer until drink time. It not only will keep the beverage icy good, but it creates a nice visual effect, too!

Fruitee Smoothie

"One for breakfast, one for lunch, and a sensible dinner." No way! I'd never want to replace a meal with any kind of shake, but this is a great one to whip up for BBQs and brunches. Be inventive with what you toss in the blender; consider seasonal fruits or even vitamin boosts. Personalize the way you serve them, too. Little paper umbrellas, fruit wedges, and edible flowers are some suggestions (could you possibly resist tossing a pansy into Uncle Todd's glass?). One pitcher serves 4 thirsty folks, so make plenty. Frozen fruit works, too, but—like Ann Blyth as "Veda Pierce"—fresher's always better!

    2 cups peaches, sliced
    1 cup blueberries
    1 cup plain yogurt (non-fat, if preferred)
    1 teaspoon lemon juice
    ¼ cup honey
    Dash of cinnamon

Puree all the ingredients until smooth as silk. Chill in the fridge (don't freeze!) or, if serving immediately, add several ice cubes when blending.

Next time you're trying to come up with a one-of-a-kind gift idea, make up an album of your recipes, liberally sprinkled with favorites from your closest friends and family. Use old photos, keepsakes, and other sentimental scrapbook items, and it will become a treasured collection that you will probably want to copy and give as gifts that are sure to be cherished. Remember that no one person has a monopoly on all the original, creative ways to entertain. It's a group effort and works best when everyone literally brings something to the table.

RECIPES FOR A BEAUTIFUL FACE AND SCALP

This one might seem good enough to eat, but it should be reserved for some night when you're home alone and in the mood for some self-beautification. My skin-care guru, Maria DeSio of Beverly Hills, has these suggestions for revitalizing yourself with some simple ingredients you probably already have available. Of course, if you're in town, why not really pamper yourself and visit Maria personally . . . capping it all off with a rejuvenating session in her hyperbaric oxygen chamber?

Cucumbers can be used for eyes to soothe and take down puffiness and swelling.

1. Peel cucumber and slice.
2. Place cucumber in refrigerator in a plastic bag.

3. Once chilled, place a cucumber slice on each eye for 20 minutes.

An egg yolk and sugar mixture can be used as a moisturizing exfoliant.

1. Mix the yolks of two eggs and a tablespoon of granulated sugar into a paste consistency.
2. Apply to face as a mask. Allow to dry.
3. Make circles on face, using fingertips, to exfoliate skin and slough off dead cells.
4. Rinse with cool water and pat dry.

Scalp treatment with onion and garlic for circulation and olive oil for split ends.

1. Peel 1 brown onion and liquefy in blender.
2. Add 1 clove of garlic to form paste.
3. Rub mixture into scalp.
4. Put plastic bag over hair for 20 minutes.
5. Rinse, then apply warmed olive oil into hair and scalp, massaging lightly.
6. Put plastic bag over hair for 20 minutes.
7. Rinse and then wash hair thoroughly.

Hmmm . . . this could explain why I get an uncontrollable craving for Italian food every time I give beautiful Maria a big hug!

"They used to photograph Shirley Temple through gauze. They should photograph me through linoleum." —TALLULAH BANKHEAD

PROPER PLACE SETTING

Eek!! Dr. Laura and John Ashcroft may espouse traditional family values, but do they know how to properly set the table?!

SAYING GOOD NIGHT

Every party has to end sooner or later, and if you put as much work into the evening as I do, you'll be pleasantly fatigued an hour or so after dessert has been polished off. Don't wait for a guest to say, "Well, it's getting late . . ."

One after-dinner drink is usually sufficient unless everyone is simply having too much fun. Be aware of conversational catch-phrases like "This has been such a great evening." That's your cue to wrap it up and perhaps make plans for the next get-together. If you're exhausted, don't leap to your feet at the first opportunity to show them the door. If all else fails, excuse yourself and duck quietly into the kitchen to do a little clean-up. It's tricky, but any savvy guest will hear that first glass clink and realize the curtain must come down. If they come in and offer to help or, God forbid, call you on it, just play innocent and say, "Oops—I got sidetracked there, sorry!"

Offering leftovers is not only generous, but a convenient method for drawing the night to a comfortable close. Keep some inexpensive plastic containers on hand to pack up to-go treats and make sure you tell your friends to keep the containers ... for a buck, you'll be remembered as benevolent Betty. By the way, don't resist sharing a recipe with an appreciative guest. Being asked is a high compliment, and anyone who's dealt with the gossip rags knows that keeping secrets only leaves the door open to suspicion and extortion!

> *Never dismiss a guest's gratitude. Being too demure is as incorrect as being conceited. When you're thanked for a lovely evening, don't poo-poo the appreciation. Instead, try something like: "I'm happy you enjoyed yourself. So did I!" Then, they won't be intimidated to invite you over sometime! (And when you accept,* Let's Dish Up a Dinner Party! *makes a charming host or hostess gift—hint, hint!)*

It's best if all your guests leave *en masse*. Otherwise, there will invariably be one or two hangers-on who will seem to want to pay rent to you rather than get out. "Fish and guests don't keep." If a nightcap doesn't give them time enough to see the light, you will have to stand up and apologize, but you're SOOOO tired and tomorrow is SUCH a big day. Employ your natural grace and tact. Like Dolly Parton says, "It's better to choose what you say, than say what you choose!" Once they're gone, you can make a mental note to save those lollygaggers for brunch dates only. Your co-host or close friends should not abandon you in these efforts and can really assist in getting Frank and Delores out the door.

You and your mate can quickly clean up whatever remaining glasses, coasters, and dishes may be lying around. Trust me, you'll be glad in the morning that you took the extra few minutes to do this.

Then, while you still have those candles lit, you might as well cuddle up on the couch and *post mortem* the evening. Give yourselves the kudos you deserve for a successful party and break up your routine: Make love right there on the couch. Your fab dinner party will end with a bang! And if it's a Party of One, that's okay, too. A job well done deserves *a hand*!

CELEBRITY DISH

No, this isn't one last recipe. It's just a few pages recounting some of my more notable star encounters from my years in show biz. These are my own personal, albeit biased, memories and impressions of some rich 'n' famous folks whose names you will surely recognize ... but the experiences and opinions expressed are *mine alone*. I'm sure some of the crankier celebs were just having a bad day, just as it's likely that some of the nicer ones were obliging a probing journalist.

I've done scores of set visits; from the lush and lighthearted atmosphere of *Will & Grace* (I auditioned for the part of "Jack." Can't you just imagine it?) to a toxic underground location deep below the Brooklyn Bridge for *Third Watch*. Also, countless at-home interviews ranging from Rodney Dangerfield's opulent high-rise condo to Betty White's cozy country Brentwood manor. People are always asking, "Who was your most memorable interview?" and "Did you ever have an affair with a movie star?" and "How bad is her face lift *really*?" and "Who's gay and who isn't?" While I may kiss, I don't usually tell, except to my best friend, Glenn. Besides, most Angelenos are so accustomed to seeing stars in the supermarket (Halle Berry is even gorgeous when buying a mop, Mike Tyson surprisingly charming), hair salons (Cloris Leachman actually pays for that look), steam rooms (Al Roker, please put the towel back on), airplanes (Yes, Whoopi, the in-flight movie really IS *Sister Act*!) and driving on the freeway (Stop tailgating me, Lily Tomlin!) that it's no big deal.

Yeah, right.

A good rule of thumb is not to believe everything you read in the tabloids, but to look for the kernel of truth on which the story is based. The three biggies (*National Enquirer, Star, Globe*) are all owned by the same publisher and they're not going to risk catastrophic law suits by reporting out and out fiction. Almost always there is a reliable, source-checked basis for their titillating reporting, which is ludicrously looked down upon by the so-called reputable entertainment magazines on sale just inches away on the newsstand shelf. Hollywood highbrows revel in gossipy dinner party conversation and it doesn't matter the source . . . it's the players who matter! Fact or fiction, the hearsay that Brad Pitt and Jennifer Aniston habitually prepare their meals in the nude makes for stimulating conversation (and the fantasy of it is probably better than the reality). Considering I knew their personal chef, the more remarkable facet of the story is that they'd cook at all!

> "Gossip is news running ahead of itself in a red satin dress."
> —LIZ SMITH.

So before we wrap things up, here's an assortment of random celebrity dish I've cooked up just for you!

Judge Judy. A tiny terminator on or off the bench, whose black robes smelled of smoke. Hollywood gets a kick out of her "New Yawk" attitude, but she needs to kick the cig habit.

Ed Begley, Jr. and Alexandra Paul. No, this isn't a *St. Elsewhere* meets *Baywatch* movie-of-the-week. These are the two most committed environmentalists in Hollywood, who really practice what they preach (unlike some A-listers who make a big deal over showing up for awards shows in chauffeur-driven hybrid cars). They recycle water, rely on solar energy, spread the message of keeping a greener planet without preaching, and even compost right in their own homes! Personally, I could never keep a box of earthworms in my kitchen, but Alexandra makes it look easy and can still manage to complete a triathlon before breakfast! And Al Unser, Jr., has nothing on Ed when he's behind the wheel of his electric vehicle. Ed'll point to his adorable baby daughter, Hayden, if you ask him why they're so committed to our planet's future. I'm quite friendly with his son, Nick, and daughter-in-law, Kyle, who are the proud new parents of a baby boy, Ellison Taylor Begley. I had them convinced to name him "Nelson" for about a nanosecond, but E.T. won out. Keep an eye peeled for the littlest Begley to be making his TV debut sometime soon!

Rebecca De Mornay. Sexy as when her hand was rocking the cradle, although the skin-tight lowriders expose more G-string than is appropriate for a PG-rated outing. She has a penchant for buying children's books, and actually pre-reading them for appropriate content.

Greg Louganis. I met the Olympic gold medalist backstage at the theater and he kindly invited me over to his place for a pool party. He still looks to be in as awesome shape as when he was diving, and his looks are only enhanced by the salt and pepper hair. I declined *immediately*! As if I'd compete against him in a swimsuit competition!

Erik Estrada. Speaking of children . . . he's a good sport, but you may be shocked to learn what's inside that locket he wears around his neck. His son's foreskin! Honest to God! Please don't share that one at the dinner table.

Melanie Griffith. Surprisingly stick-thin, obviously thanks to the smokes hanging out of her back pocket. She should look to her fabulous mother, *The Birds* star Tippi Hedren, as a role model for poise, gentility, and aging gracefully. I suspect most of the stories we hear about Mel are true, considering the brusque (i.e. rude) reception I received from her while visiting her mother's home. "Don't look at me!" she shrieked. (Can you fathom behaving like that in *your* mother's house?!) Tippi's Shambala Wild Animal Preserve is one of the must-experience landmarks in Southern California, and the Tip-ster is its radiant hostess. She even has a magnificent tent overlooking the elephant sanctuary, complete with a king-sized bed for overnight guests! In Melanie's own home, which happens to be a few blocks away from mine, she and Antonio keep pretty much to themselves (no elephants), but you know how gossip gets over the garden gate!

Lucie Arnaz. She didn't like it when I pointed out that she in no way resembles either of her parents. She's tall, thin, and has bright green eyes. Maybe she's part Mertz?

Anne Heche. No matter what side of the sexual fence she is on, or what alien experiences she may claim to have had, she is arguably the greatest actress of her generation and has always been a friendly, supportive star ever since we worked on *Another World* together way back in the eighties. I know what Ellen saw in her . . . she's an amazing kisser (unlike a certain slobbering *West Wing* star, wig-wearing Broadway director, *Titanic*-featured actor who put the "bite" in "bit player," or teeth-banging *Smallville* actor, who shall all remain nameless).

Judd Nelson. The big brother I always wanted. An enthusiastic guy's guy who's not afraid to throw his arm over my shoulder every time he sees me and enthuse, "You know, if we got married, you'd be *Nelson Nelson*!"

Jeff Goldblum. For my money, still the sexiest guy in Hollywood and with more real movie star quality than any of his contemporaries. Eye contact, firm handshake, charm for days, multitalented, natty dresser. The first time we met, I had to venture a guess (as soon as I could catch my breath) that he was not a pet owner. Why? There was not a speck on his immaculate black suit, *anywhere.* What a refreshing change from his grungy contemporaries and, yes, I do have it on tape that he called me "beautiful." Now you know what made Geena Davis and Laura Dern fall so hard!

Blind item: Betcha can't guess which African-American TV personality said, "Nelson's just my type; short, white, and feisty!"

Faye Dunaway. The terror of Tinseltown for over thirty years and counting. She makes Shannen Doherty look like a rank amateur. No sales clerk, movie usher, or flight attendant is safe from her legendary outbursts and demands. I've personally suffered through her tirades in a furniture store and an aerobic studio. If you see her coming, drop the wire hanger and escape to the nearest exit.

Robert Reed. Yes, I did know Mr. Brady, but not in the Biblical sense. We worked on *Search for Tomorrow* together and went to a few of the same parties. I've spent years looking for his younger off-screen counterpart. Sadly, that's when one has to grow up and accept the fact that *The Brady Bunch* wasn't real. (Keep reading for more Brady news and a couple of Partridges out of the pear tree, too.)

Doris Roberts. This Emmy winner is *everywhere.* I'm sure if you invite her for dinner, she will be there!

Dick Van Dyke. One of the great ones and best interview subject, ever. Smart, self-effacing, and a gentleman. This town is tough on anyone over forty and he's managed to thrive, not just survive, and still be as happy and friendly as you'd imagine him to be! This good sport also sings in his own barbershop quartet, appropriately named "The Vantastix"!

Audience feedback. Since, aside from the occasional cameo role as a reporter in TV and film, my on-air appearances are not "acting," per se, the kind of response I get from audiences is generally friendly and supportive (if you don't count the fact that I am repeatedly informed that I am much shorter in person). Unlike the soap opera villain who gets hissed at in the deli, or the heartthrob who gets stalked in the subway, folks who recognize and appreciate my contributions to the world of entertainment usually offer a wave, an amicable greeting, or blow a kiss. Lois, my Springer spaniel, evokes more passionate responses thanks to her frequent co-starring spots with me, having been spotted by dog-delirious hikers in the canyons of Hollywood, and having received poochie-personal parcels in the mail. Fellow animal owners kindly share photos and stories of their own pampered pets, although neither Lois nor I ever eat any food received in the mail. Pre-recorded singing birthday cards are cute and some personalized oven mitts are proudly hung up near the oven. Once, after hosting a series of PBS pledge break specials with funnyman Bruce Vilanch, one viewer wrote me to contest my use of the term "sexual preference" in terms of describing sexuality. He rightly pointed out that by saying "preference," one implies *choice*, something most gays do not believe is a factor in determining their sexuality. I appreciated and agreed with his comment and now use "sexual orientation" instead. Makes sense, eh? And in all my years of celebrity news wrangling, I've never had a complaint or dispute . . . with one exception. When I reported on live radio that curvaceous Carmen Electra was dating basketball star Dennis Rodman, she quickly called in to the station to dispute the charge. While I was glad to know she was an attentive listener to my program, I was even happier when news of their courtship hit the mainstream press and I was proven right. Hey, if I can't back it up, I won't bother talking about it!

Sweet fan mail from an open-minded female viewer: "Don't know your age, but you seem very young in a mature way . . . and it's all the better that you are gay 'cause like one adores a painting/dress/house/landscape, I am like that with people. Can't help admiring beauty of both sexes, and why not? If a gorgeous weather girl's beauty brightens up a few moments for me, I think people realize I'm just admiring something lovely and I can get away with it more with gay men 'cause others know it isn't a sexual thing." Love that!

Kathy Ireland. This model-turned-mogul is now a ubiquitous "lifestyles expert." And you're sternly warned against referring to her as an "ex" anything. Wait a minute . . . she was never a model?!

The gym. Hands down the best venue for seeing stars in their most unguarded moments. Most of them actually look better in person. Jason Priestley, for example, looks great. Julia Roberts does not. Dixie Carter looks and acts just like her on-screen self. Mindy Cohn and William H. Macy are extremely athletic (who knew?!). Alfred Molina, sweating on the giant core-stabilizer ball, is something to see. Annette Bening can do about a zillion leg lifts, seemingly without the slightest perspiration. Magic Johnson oozes charisma whether he's lifting weights with his buddies or shooting hoops with other gym-goers. Kristin Davis, Alfre Woodard, Belita Moreno, Lolita Davidovitch, Margeaux Hemingway, Ashley Judd, Helen Hunt, Craig Bierko, Carol Kane, Lauralee Bell, and Pia Zador-able all took my fitness classes back in my *Perfect* aerobic days.

Debbie Reynolds. On assignment, I got to spend a weekend at the hotel and casino owned by this silver screen legend. Arguably the hardest-working dame in showbiz and as emotionally facile as anyone I've ever met. Although she's as "on" as her fictional alter-ego in *Postcards from the Edge*, she shared lots of personal stories in our interview and proudly showed off her collection of movie wardrobe items. The casino was not to be believed . . . images of Debbie were *everywhere*. Even on the slot machines! Three "Debbies" and you were a winner! Too bad the place finally went belly up . . . but she's still workin' on stage and on screen. Leg up! Did you know her closest gal celeb pal was Agnes "Endora" Moorehead?

Dining out. Hey, even celebrities have to eat. In Hollywood, the caliber and quality of the restaurant is usually on par with the level of celebrity you're likely to encounter at the next table. Casual Carribean for Ellen DeGeneres . . . high-end Italian for Spielberg and Capshaw, Isabella Rossellini, and Ralph Fiennes . . . Beverly Hills bistro fare for Sally Field, and fast food drive-thru for David Spade. But what on earth does Lucy Liu see in a popular gay Mexican cantina?! Thank goodness for a hangover brunch at the Fiddler's Diner, or I'd never have gotten to flirt with Wesley Eure (remember teen-idol "Will" from *Land of the Lost*?).

Film festivals. Hollywood loves to pat itself on the back. Every five minutes there's a gala to honor someone and usually the old guard will come out in force to pay tribute. These are unbeatable occasions not only to schmooze with an eclectic coterie of film fans (where else would a Texan madam with a *Gone With the Wind* obsession wind up at the same table with a Trekkie?), but to hang out with the very idols who still dazzle us with stars in our eyes! I've had great chats with Rod Steiger (his all-time favorite book? *Le Petit Prince*. Although, in fairness, he didn't live to see *this* one's publication), Olivia De Havilland, King Vidor, Glenn Ford, Evelyn Keyes, Nina Foch, Betty Garrett, Jane Russell, John Saxon, Ann Miller, Cliff Robertson, and let's not forget over-the-top Mamie Van Doren! I even sang a little duet from *L'il Abner* with darling dynamo Edie Adams. What stories they tell and told! You want

conversation at your next dinner party? Make sure to invite someone over the age of sixty. You're sure to learn something fascinating!

Camp classics. As a child of the TV generation, I appreciate anyone who ever sat on a game show panel or whose face adorned one
of my many school lunch boxes. Most of them are still in town and
many are doing interesting things you never read about at the
checkout stand. Renee Taylor has a one-woman show about Golda
Meir! Lee Meriwether, aside from finding the Fountain of Youth,
performs serious drama. Polly Bergen can sure belt out a tune when
she's not bumming smokes. Lois Nettleton, Clarence Williams III,
Marcia Wallace, Deborah Van Valkenburgh, Wil Wheaton, Elvira,
Hulk Hogan, sweet Nancy Sinatra ("Nelson, the day I met you, I
must have had an angel sitting on my shoulder!") and Deanna
"Banana" Lund are not just answers in Trivial Pursuit. These people are still out there and they're *fabulous*! Who knew Ron Palillo,
TV's "Horshack," would turn out so good looking or Mimi Rogers,
Dr. Ruth, or JoBeth Williams so playful? In fact, Robert Vaughn
called on his *Man from U.N.C.L.E.* celebrity to help my British
friend Alexandra out of a jam when they held us at the Canadian
border (Silly, she had forgotten her pesky passport!), causing us to
miss our flight out of Buffalo, a place from which you do not want to
miss your flight. He was a real hero! Shirley Jones may still look
just like Shirley Partridge, but she confesses to a strange side even
darker than her Oscar-winning role in *Elmer Gantry*: She is a true-
crime buff and can't get enough gory books on serial killers! Come
on, all you TV Movie Development Execs . . . start pitching Shirley
as Ma Barker!

Danny Bonaduce. The plump redheaded Partridge survived his
"wild child" twenties and is now a successful, responsible (and
buff!) TV and radio personality, whom I've interviewed many times
for several different mediums. And he's a man of his word! On the
air during a live radio interview, he bet me twenty bucks I wouldn't
know the answer to his trivia question: "In what movie was the
first openly gay reference by a major movie star?" Tsk, tsk, Danny.

I quickly snapped back, "Cary Grant in *Bringing Up Baby*, wearing a woman's peignoir, exclaims, 'I've suddenly gone *gay!*'" He paid up on the spot. When a listener called in to espouse his own opinion about how EVERY man is secretly queer, I countered with my Friction Theory. Okay, class, take notes! A dog will mount your leg or the arm of your sofa not because it is physically attracted to said limb or furnishing. It is because the friction *feels good*. This does not make your dog into a pervert. Get the connection? Add that to the fact that the male genitalia is on the outside of his body and susceptible to all kinds of friction. . . . well, that doesn't make someone gay! Just because a guy's gay-friendly, doesn't mean he's a closet case. Danny would agree—he's straight, but a great friend to the gay community.

> "*Even Mel Gibson, Brad Pitt, and Russell Crowe, all presumably straight, are in fact personally unknown to their adoring fans.*"
> —RICHARD CHAMBERLAIN, ACTOR
> AND AUTHOR OF *Shattered Love*

Sally Kirkland's Boobs. That pair has received more worldwide press, both good and bad, than the Olson Twins. Vivacious, Golden Globe–winning Sally is the sweetheart of most reporters because she will always give 200 percent. When I was writing an article on the then-impending removal of her controversial (and enormous) silicone breast implants, she made sure my research was literally *hands on*. Suffice it to say, she hosted the interview from her giant and admittedly comfortable bed in her West Hollywood *pied a terre* and I got a firsthand look—and feel—at her surgeon's handiwork.

Christopher Reeve. The real Superman! As amazing as you think he is when you see him in interviews, he is ten times greater in person. In spite of the daunting physical obstacles and overwhelming inconveniences involved in orchestrating any appearance he makes (think medical and security), he manages to be patient, focused, articulate, and good humored. I worked with him in Niagara Falls in the late nineties and it was impossible not to be moved and inspired by his courage and determination. He can certainly be forgiven for that third *Superman* sequel.

Leeza Gibbons. Don't be fooled by all the pancake and lip gloss, she's as sharp and together off camera as she is on. Brainy, quick-witted, charming and a real pro in command of any situation. She adores the spotlight but excels just as easily behind the scenes. Although it may seem like she'd show up for the opening of even a cereal box, this dame is one potent powder puff!

Gloria Gaynor. Her husband/manager, Linwood Simon, chain smokes at any opportunity and it doesn't seem to bother the Disco Diva in the least . . . even before a performance in a windowless Green Room. Gives new meaning to *I Will Survive!*

Florence Henderson. It may surprise you to know that Mrs. Brady is also a licensed hypnotherapist. It surprised me even more when I interviewed her on the subject and she revealed her belief that someone could be hypnotized *out* of being gay! She must not have tried it on the *Brady* set, and I sure wouldn't want her trying it on me!

9-11. Since everyone wonders where everyone else was on 9-11, I'll tell you my story. I was on location for the Lifetime Annie Potts series *Any Day Now,* playing the part of a scandal-sniffing life-styles reporter (typecast again!) covering a Civil War Memorial in a cemetery. My trailer had one of the few televisions, so you can just imagine the added strangeness of an already surreal experi-ence: scores of extras clad in antebellum costumes crowding in to watch the events unfold and listen for updates. Surprisingly, per-haps thankfully, the "show must go on," and shooting proceeded as scheduled. It didn't require much acting talent to portray solemnity in the graveyard that day.

Chita's. Ahh, to be in your twenties, living in New York City ! So many nights Glenn and I would sweep in and stagger out! This was Broadway legend Chita Rivera's cool restaurant on West 42nd Street long before the neighborhood's revitalization or leopard-print upholstery became *en vogue*. It was haunted by the most dramatic denizens Hell's Kitchen had to offer and star-sightings were as common as souvenir *Playbills* . . . Billy Stritch played piano to a swooning (I think she was swooning!) Liza with a "Z." Oh, look! There's Michael Feinstein coming from a suspected make-out session in the restroom. Over there: Henny Youngman bellowing from a corner table, "Chita! Chita!" only to be told that the hostess is actually Chita's lookalike sister, Lola. Unfazed, he continues with, "Chita's Sister! Chita's sister!"

Runyon Canyon Dog Park. Want to see how the stars treat their four-legged friends? Who pooper scoops and who looks the other way? Head up there and you're likely to run into George Clooney, Kyle MacLachlan, Danny DeVito and Rhea Perlman, Linda Evangelista, CCH Pounder, Mary Stuart Masterson, Dorothy Lyman, or Tanya Roberts (what a striking sight to see Sheena, Queen of the Jungle, charging through the craggy passes with her magnificent Dobermans!). And there are all those aspiring young hotties looking for their big breaks, while trying to look like they're not looking!

Kitty-Kat Tea Parties. I wouldn't have believed it, if I hadn't seen it with my own eyes. If you're not a dog person, hook up with Carol Connors (see her Carat Cake recipe on pages 119–20) for one of her elegantly catered feline festivals. Not only does she set up a purr-fectly divine catered tea party to honor her pet Abyssinian, Lyrics, her Beverly Hills guest list includes celebrity pals like Barbi Benton, Marilyn McCoo, Charlene Tilton, Kate Linder, and Rhonda Shear . . . actually clad in cat-print couture and arriving with animal-themed gifts! Apparently, Julie Newmar and Eartha Kitt don't like to play along. Their loss! These ladies are cat-tastic! I was so inspired that I hired a stripper to help celebrate my puss, Henry's, tenth birthday. You can just imagine his surprise (the stripper's, not the cat's!).

My stage career. I told you about my humble beginnings playing a pig, but my adult career off and way-off Broadway was no less un-glamorous. Luncheon theater for busloads of senior citizens got me my Equity card and taught me a lot about singing with a hangover. Dinner theater for busloads of senior citizens led to eligibility for Unemployment and taught me a lot about curing hangovers. Incidentally, the thought of my posh, bejeweled friend Marcia McCabe (*Search for Tomorrow*'s scrappy "Sunny Adamson") accompanying me to the Manhattan unemployment office in her full-length mink coat is one of my all time favorite memories . . . it always reminds me to hold my head up high in any situation! All along the not-so-White Way, I got to emote with stars in all stages of their career arcs. How else could I have played half of Patrick Duffy's horse (the *front* half, thank you) in *The Taming of the Shrew*, Charleston'ed with "Titus" actor David Shatraw in *The Boyfriend*, kissed *Sordid Lives* hunk Kirk Geiger in *Burn This*, been harassed by Tony-winner Dorothy Loudon's midnight phone calls, sung "Makin' Whoopee" on both Arlene Francis's and Joey Adams's radio shows, done a script reading with Richard Dreyfuss playing my father, or gotten to appear alongside my then-favorite soap star Lezlie Dalton on the ultra-camp "Joe Franklin Show"!? I even got to make a very funny movie spoof of "Mommie Dearest," now in the hands of "Everybody Loves Raymond's" Monica Horan ("Amy") and her husband, executive producer Phil Rosenthal— hopefully they've got it under lock and key! I keep waiting for the extortion letter to arrive in the mail one of these days.

Mommie

Acting 101. The best TV acting tip I ever got was from *One Life to Live* leading man, James DePaiva. For decades he's been playing "Max Holden" and, on an almost daily basis for thousands of episodes, he's had to emote for the camera as a scene slowly fades to a tampon or deodorant commercial. He told me the best way to fill that seemingly interminable gap of time was to "pretend you're smelling something really bad." Try it, right now. He's absolutely correct—that pinched expression you're wearing will work for a myriad emotions. Confusion. Intrigue. Disgust. Thoughtfulness. Skepticism.

> *"All anyone in Hollywood can ever think of is publicity, box office, movies, scripts. Why don't any of you ever try to understand a woman?"* —FROM THE SCREENPLAY *Mommie Dearest*, BY FRANK YABLANS, FRANK PERRY, AND ABRAHAM POLONSKY

"Nelson's World." This was a live talk show I produced and hosted for MSN in the late nineties. 186 one-hour episodes of interviews that briefly made me the Larry King of the Internet. Some celebrities certainly put my hosting skills to the test. Ruby Wax was anything but *Absolutely Fabulous.* She showed up late and criticized everything. Sadly, Sir Ian McKellan was a last-minute cancellation. John Schneider's political views were so *Dukes of Hazzard,* I was dumbfounded. Carol Alt displayed less than model behavior by scheduling another appearance back to back. Cute Soleil Moon Frye came with an uninvited guest (a happy break: Danny Masterson was a charmer!). Laura Leighton simply *had* to have her dog with her. I guess they didn't allow pets at Melrose Place. The late author Marcel Montecino used blue language the whole time. Leave It to Jerry Mathers to whine and complain *and* arrive over an hour early! Holy Letdown! Bawdy Burt Ward threatened to be a no-show at the last minute and instead only phoned in his interview. Usually glamorous Connie Selleca was fun, but surprisingly dressed down—didn't put on any makeup and just wore a T-shirt. Vanessa Marcil nearly put me in *General Hospital* after requesting a strictly vegan menu in the greenroom. On the other hand, most were delights. Miss Universe let me try on her sash! Ed McMahon knew from experience exactly how to keep a conversation going. *Batman* creator Bob Kane let his wife do the talking while he effortlessly captivated company by cartooning the Caped Crusader! (He did share an interesting tidbit: he believed George Clooney was the best casting of any Bruce Wayne. Do you agree?) Mink Stole the show with a litany of Divine recollections. Downtown Julie Brown brought a gift. David Boreanaz, Kevin Nealon, hunky Greg Evigan, Esai Morales, Sidney Sheldon, Julia Sweeney, LeVar Burton, John Woo (in spite of the language barrier), Caroll Baker, and Jackie Collins all possessed memorable *elan* and sportsmanship. Penthouse Pet and B-movie queen Julie Strain lived up to her autobiography; she really *is* "6'1, and Worth the Climb!" Joan van Ark *is* as skinny as you think, but even nicer than her "Val Ewing" alter ego. The legendary master of hosting, Steve Allen, proved that there's always room for newcomers by being gracious and as interest*ed* as he was interest*ing*! Sultry Andrea Thompson and Jill Hennessey tie for first place for combining *naughty* and *nice*! Casey Kasem implored me in the voice of Scooby-Doo's "Shaggy" to quit smoking . . . and I did! How could I let him down after *that*!? Edward James Olmos knows how to flatter a host: he claimed I was "the best he ever worked with!" Aww, shucks . . .

"The worst part of success is to try finding someone who is happy for you."
                                                    —BETTE MIDLER

New with Nelson! This was a series of minute-long "Infotainment" segments I produced for the in-store televisions at Ralph's chain of Southern California supermarkets. For over a year, grocery shoppers were assaulted 24/7 with my How-To tidbits while they stood in line. Ten million people a month were force-fed my useful programming, which ranged from creative lighting for your backyard party to veterinary tips and installing a dimmer switch (so butch!). Along the way, I got to play with Susan Anton, Charles Durning, Ed Asner, Marcia Wallace, Marion Ross, David Hasselhoff, Alan Thicke, Sid Caesar, Isabel Sanford, sexy Charlotte Ross and her one-eyed dog named Katie, Michael Madsen, the late Robert Stack, Martin Landau, Jamie Foxx, Lorna Luft, John Corbett, and Bo Derek. It afforded me a strange kind of recognition, with people not knowing why I seemed familiar to them. When they'd stare or comment on the fact that they thought they knew me from *somewhere*, I'd usually just shrug and ask, "Paper or plastic?"

Billy Dee Williams. I met Billy Dee at a Christmas Eve dinner party in Beverly Hills. The strangest thing: No one was talking to him! I figured it was because he was the only celebrity in the room (the score was roughly Uptight White People: 10; Homosexuals: 2; Celebrities: 1) so I started chatting him up about his painting, which I'd heard was one of his many talents. It wasn't long before everyone was gathered around us, asking questions and participating in the conversation. It was not unlike hosting "Inside the Actor's Studio," and I realized how vital it is to make sure your guest list includes at least one conversationalist to act as a facilitator when needed! Incidentally, Billy Dee has told me on more than one occasion that he wants to paint my portrait, and I am still waiting. After all, Dorian Gray I am not, so hurry up, Lando Calrissian!

Odd Jobs. While working toward my TV journalism career I did—as most actors do (think *That Girl!*)—an assortment of strange survival jobs. Taking dictation was first. A disaster when I sent out a surgeon's letter about a patient's "Below Knee Amputation" but spelled it: "Bologna" Amputation. I just assumed it was a procedure introduced by an Italian physician. Script typing was even worse. A TV actress was directed to react as if "the ultimate *horror* was bestowed." Turns out, I'd misread the executive producer's handwritten notes. It should have been "the ultimate *honor* bestowed." Very opposite interpretations from the actress who, incidentally, agreed with my take on it! At least I wasn't pigeonholed in that career (Marcia McCabe nicknamed me *Nimble Finger Nels* and it stuck!). Caricaturing at kids' birthday parties ... dressing as a bunny rabbit for a tea-pot trade show in Rockefeller Center's swell-egant Rainbow Room ... spraying cologne for horribly spoiled children at F.A.O. Schwarz ... teaching "Sit 'n' Fit" for senior citizens ... hosting at Mezzaluna Restaurant (yes, I knew Nicole Simpson) ... calling out the numbers with a charismatic cross-dresser named Belle Aire at "Drag Queen Bingo." But once you've "made it," the assignments are often even stranger: Boxing with Michelle Phillips, Looping with Lee Grant, Fairy School, Doggie Weddings, Celebrity Slumber Parties, Margarita Pedicures or Painting with Body Parts. Just the other day I was reporting from in front of Madonna's Beverly Hills compound on Roxbury and remembering how many times I'd used her song *Vogue* as a cooldown routine for a low impact groove dance class I taught in my salad days. Thanks to that dance craze, I actually got to private coach the late Broadway legend Gwen Verdon one summer in Westhampton, Long Island. As was proven in her two *Cocoon* movies, she was still as sexy in a black leotard when a senior citizen as she was in her provocative cover pose on the Original Cast Album of *Sweet Charity*. Man—never say no to an opportunity. You never know where it will take you!

Celebrity journalism. Who says showbiz reporting is all fluff stuff? I've had demanding and challenging assignments ranging from Oscar coverage during the Iraqi war and the great Katharine

Hepburn's death to the murder/suicide of Mr. & Mrs. Phil Hartman and every new Michael Jackson controversy. These stories are important to the public, so reporting them intelligently and accurately is important to *me*. And once in a while, I get to do a little investigative work! I've gone undercover as an NBC studio page, a Power Ranger, and a Jeopardy contestant (the toughest part really is commandeering that little hand buzzer). . . .

The Poseidon Adventure. For some odd reason (and I know I'm not alone!), it's my all-time favorite movie and as strangely quotable as *All About Eve*. Over the years, I've had the pleasure of participating in various Poseidon-related screenings, panels and events all over North America. I've even gotten to interview and party with many of its cast and crew including Ernest Borgnine, Red Buttons, Carol Lynley, Roddy McDowell, Stella Stevens (look! Someone came in costume as "Linda's enema!"), Pamela Sue Martin, Sheila (Mrs. Irwin) Allen, Costumer Paul Zastupnevich and Director Ronald Neame. Whether it was riding the Maid of the Mist with Carol beneath Niagara Falls, having my thigh squeezed by Roddy as he watched himself onscreen—plunging to his death in a flooded shaft, or reenacting Robin & Susan's camp "shove it" scene with Pamela Sue on the deck of the *Queen Mary*, it's one film that has certainly had an ongoing effect in my life. Maybe you should screen it at your next New Year's Eve party! In spite of the Seventies styles, it still stands up!

> *"I saw a young officer on deck the other day and he looked pretty damned familiar. Even with his clothes on!"*
> —STELLA STEVENS (as Linda Rogo, *The Poseidon Adventure*, screenplay by Sterling Silliphant)

Survivor **host Jeff Probst.** So incredibly matinee-idol handsome in person, with a picturesque little house perfectly decorated from the pages of the Pottery Barn catalogue! Who *wouldn't* want to be stranded with him on a deserted island?!

Still to interview. Celebrities remaining on my wish list include Stevie Nicks, Paul Newman, Liza Minnelli (I told you I love disaster movies), Johnny Carson, Elizabeth Taylor, Vincent Bugliosi (Shirley Jones ain't the only true-crime buff!), Johnny Depp, Julianne Moore (loved her playing twins on "As the World Turns"; who needs an Oscar!?), Julia Child, Brendan Fraser, Jennifer Saunders, Ed Norton (he and Courtney Love used to sit around and read poetry together!), and my favorite TV chef, dreamboat Tyler Florence.

CLOSING THOUGHTS

Whether you live in a studio apartment or a sprawling house with a 500-square foot kitchen, the ability to throw a fab dinner party is within your grasp. I learned from my on-air hosting and interview experiences that the important components of off-air hosting are the same no matter what side of the camera you're sitting on. Be generous and opt for laughter whenever possible.

There's no occasion too small to merit celebrating. Back when I was just a little boy, my mom and I declared on a whim that every March 19 would be "Nelson & Mother's Day," and we still do something special to acknowledge it annually. Why not invent *your* own holiday? My friend Liz decorates sheet cakes with silly little items from the dollar store, cleverly conceived to reflect the personality of the guest of honor. Her "Kooky Kakes" are a treasured tradition in our circle! How about if you fete your friends the next time they get a raise at work or do something special to warmly welcome them home after their next vacation? Check the Internet for "On This Day in History" to come up with a momentous occasion if you don't already have one of your own. You may never have imagined how much fun it is to commemorate the anniversary of the Beatles arriving in America or make a Baked Alaska on the same day that Alaska became a state!

Want to know the secret of Wolfgang Puck's success? When you're eating at Spago, notice the attention to detail lavished on every item on *and* off the table. So much thought is given that you can't help but feel special, whether he's there to personally greet you, or not. Do the same when you invite people into your home.

Organize what you can control and be ready for anything you can't. The more often you throw these soirees, the more inventive and confident you'll become. And when you latch on to new ideas, write and tell me so I can include you in volume 2: "Let's Dish Up *Another* Dinner Party!"

NELSON'S LITTLE BLACK BOOK

Y ou didn't really think I'd give out the information from my *real* little black book, did you? That's private and confidential! When it comes to romance, I can't help but be proprietary (That former *90210* hottie is mine, all mine! Why do you suppose I took up tennis, for the exercise?! I'm keeping that dashing CNN anchor's private line to myself, too!). As far as dinner parties go, however, I'm more than happy to share! Proving that the Internet isn't just a great tool for dating, I'm including website addresses so you can research ways to customize your own dining event with these wonderful resources. Google is my preferred search engine—you can find just about anything to make your day; maybe even a long lost love or the obituary of that third-grade teacher who's still giving you nightmares.

Safe handling. I'm a chronic hand-washer and counter-cleaner, and if anything I'm prone to overcooking rather than risk the dangers of undercooking. So I use the Cook'd Right instant poultry sensors from Segan Industries. They're fast and accurate, disposable devices for checking your chicken and pork temperatures. In fact, for everything you've always wanted to know about poultry but were afraid to ask, visit the very helpful website of the California Poultry Federation at www.cpif.org. You'll be surprised how many fowl facts you'll find!

Wine 'n' dine. My fellow Hofstra alumnus Francis Ford Coppola is best known for his *Godfather* movies, but in my house it's all about his fantastic wines. You must check out www.neibaum-coppola.com, which I discovered while a member of his excellent wine club. I hope to someday take a luxurious and liquid vacation at his Napa Valley vineyards. In the meantime, I *always* keep plenty of his table red and white labels ready for consumption. The Rosso combines Cabernet Sauvignon, Syrah, and Zinfandel in a just-sweet-enough blend. And every afternoon around 5 p.m., my mouth waters for the Sauvignon Blanc, Chardonnay, and Pinot Grigio–composed Bianco. Learn more at www.rossobianco.com. I wager you'll love them as much as I do!

Has your home town been lucky enough to get a Trader Joe's Market, yet? All sorts of gourmet goodies and bargain wines from these merry merchants! You can always sneak a peek at www.traderjoes.com.

www.cheese.com offers 700-plus varieties of cheese that can be shipped fresh to your door. They also have a vast selection of *accoutrements du fromage* such as knives, melters, cutting boards, fondue pots, and cheese makers. Your mouth will water!

When you've decided on some cheese, surf on over to www.pepperfood.com and find out everything you ever wanted to dis-

cover about absolutely *every* kind of pepper. There are also re-
views, recipes, products, and myriad links to other spicy sites.

Kitchen supplies. In nearby Culver City is Surfas, a restaurant
supply house and kitchen design business founded in 1937 that
touts itself as a "chef's paradise." They also have gourmet food and
product catalogues so that everyone can become a patron. Whether
it's a butcher-block table on wheels, a professional pizza oven, or
simply a new spatula, you're sure to spot something you can't live
without! Online, they're at www.surfasonline.com. 8825 National
Boulevard, Culver City, CA. 90232. (310) 559-4770.

You already know about the sick attachment I feel toward my
stupendous Williams Sonoma bread machine, but I also feel a tingly
sensation for several of their other more reasonably priced staples.
The dishtowels are perfect, and I always pick up a pack even if I'm
just in the store to browse. The fragrant kitchen soaps with matching hand creams in the handy pump dispensers are also must-
haves. I particularly like the ones with essential rosemary oils.
Why not have a little aromatherapy, even when you're not cooking? www.williams-sonoma.com

Whether it's Maypo, Beeman's Gum, or My-T-Fine pie filling,
you'll want to visit www.hometownfavorites.com for a *literal* taste
of nostalgia! They have long-discontinued food products from your
childhood that will bring back delicious (or not-so-delicious, as your
now-adult tastebuds may prove!) memories.

Check out the "Gold Box" on www.amazon.com *and find unexpected, constantly changing bargains. You might get lucky and find the cocktail napkins, knife sharpener, or melon-baller you keep forgetting to buy! There's so much more than books!*

Decorating. I'm a total slut when it comes to shopping around for *tchotchkes*, and my very favorite places are probably in your hometown, too. Pier 1 Imports (www.pier1.com), Cost Plus World Markets (www.costplus.com), Crate and Barrel (www.crateand barrel.com), and Pottery Barn (www.potterybarn.com) always have great discounts on candles, chargers, placemats, stemware, vases, table linens, picture frames, place card holders, door mats, and so on, especially in their Clearance sections! That enables you to constantly rejuvenate or replenish your collections to reflect the changes in season or even the themes of your parties. Since they're national chain stores, you can check out the websites before you shop to see what kinds of discounts you can actually expect to find on the shelves.

Setting the table. I told you earlier about Replacements Ltd., the ultimate outlet for finding old and new china, silver, collectibles, and more. Their motto is "We replace the irreplaceable!" Call 1-800-REPLACE [737-5223] or go online to www.replacementsltd.com; 1089 Knox Road, Greensboro, NC 26029.

Bed, Bath and Beyond has a little bit of everything and always seems to have a thing or two you'll realize you desperately need. If you have an outlet in your neighborhood, it also makes for a convenient place to find a reasonably priced hostess gift, whether it's a decorative bottle of olive oil or luxurious bath set. Of course, you

can check out the merchandise on their website, www.bedbathand
beyond.com. They're also great about honoring discount coupons
from competitors!

Recipes. Look, guilty or innocent, Martha Stewart is undeniably
a goddess, but I can't and won't spin sugar in my spare time. Besides, I don't have her support staff to clean up the resulting mess.
That cute Rachel Ray on the Food Network's *30-Minute Meals* is
more my style: user friendly and bubbly (and she gets a gold star
for neatness and cleanliness!), so with that in mind I usually avoid
cookbooks and prefer to get my guidelines from websites such as
www.foodtv.com, www.cooking.com, and www.epicurious. com.

Author Alan Jacobson turned me on to www.drweil.com, which
has endless healthy recipes, complete with nutritional breakdowns.
As a sort-of assignment to keep my culinary chops honed, I'll buy
the latest issue of *Gourmet* or *Food and Wine* magazines, and select one new recipe to try out. It's fun, and my friends (almost) always enjoy being guinea pigs for these experimental evenings!

If you're still a fan of the traditional cookbook, however, you
should consider the book clubs available through www.thegood-
cook.com and www.jessicasbiscuit.com.

www.smartsource.com has plenty of recipes and, if you're a clip-
per like me, coupons to print and redeem. It admittedly leans toward the low-end of the gastronomic cooking scale, but does have
some clever tips that you may want to adapt for your own kitchen
uses. Turning "scraps of a nice cotton dress" into napkins or "sponge
painting an old sheet to use as a tablecloth" are *not* among them.

Who says English food is awful? No matter which side of the
pond you're on, you can enjoy one of the U.K.'s most popular retail
outlets, Marks and Spencer, by logging on to their website,
www.marksand spencer.com. Check out their Food Magazine page,
which has lots of useful information and an especially good link to
sources for Indian cuisine.

Buy in bulk! If you're serious about your spices, dried fruits,
beans, grains, candies, or nuts, check out the amazing world of Torn
and Glasser in downtown Los Angeles. My friend Greg Glasser is

passionate about his family business and supplies retailers with the freshest and tastiest imaginable! www.tornandglasser.com; 1622 East Olympic Blvd., Los Angeles, CA 90021; (213) 627-6496.

Specialty items. English goodies like Lion Bars, Birds Custard, or Branston's Pickle can be tough to find, but Ye Olde King's Head has a British Shoppe that you Anglophiles can visit in person or online. 116 Santa Monica Blvd., Santa Monica, CA 90401; (310) 394-8765; www.yeoldekingshead.com.

My pal Chef Olivier Quinn pointed me toward www.dean deluca.com for gourmet supplies and I was most impressed by their section of gift suggestions and corporate gifts. Super useful for those of you with a corporate budget! He also turned me on to www.kingarthurflour.com, based in Norwich, Vermont. If whatever you're doing has anything to do with baking, they can probably help you. Their toll-free number is (800) 827-6836.

And speaking of special, if the meat at your market just doesn't make the grade, log on to www.dartagnan.com and check out what they have on special. It might be worth becoming a member if you want to always be sure to have the freshest quality paté, foie gras, sausages, organic game, and smoked delicacies. 280 Wilson Avenue, Newark, NJ 07105; (800) 327-8246.

Stationery. I was delighted to discover www.horchow.com for stationery. The importance and thoughtfulness of sending lovely invitations and/or thank-you notes can never be overestimated. They also have departments such as Tabletops & Table Linens and Seasonal & Gourmet, both worth checking out.

Assorted what-nots and tips. Mind your manners and brush up on your dinner party do's and don'ts by visiting www.emilypost.com.

"I took tips and was glad to get them."
—JOAN CRAWFORD AS "MILDRED PIERCE"

Is it a fortuitous time to be entertaining? Make like former First Lady Nancy Reagan and check out your forecast at www. astrology-online.com. It's also a fun source for coming up with creative, personalized place settings or games.

Looking for something fun to serve or bring as a hostess gift? Maybe a chocolate handbag or one of the other novelties from www.chocochocohouse.com ("Where Chocolate Meets Fashion") is the answer.

What happened on this day in history? www.historychannel. com will tell you, in case you want to create a relevant theme for your party. Maybe Beverly Cohn's www.4perfectgifts.com will help you devise some appropriate party favors to go along with the times you are paying tribute to!

On the subject of themes, my sister's monthly card group always antes up their Gin Rummy pot for a local charity. Maybe you're feeling philanthropic and want to do the same for your next dinner party. Have everyone bring a donation to a particular organization, food bank, or Good Will outlet. When I'm raising money for my AIDS marathons, I'll throw special dinner party events expressly for my biggest donors. If your hosting reputation is impressive, you might just do very well! And it's tax deductible. To research organizations by type (human rights, disease, etc.) or region (local, international), look at www.takingitglobal.org. Have a dinner party that makes a difference!

When it comes to gifts and novelties, aahs! is a popular Hollywood shop with several locations. They now offer a large selection of their silly stuff for online purchase as well. Visit www.aahs.com or call (310) 829-1807.

Remember I told you how nice it is to give the gift of an inscribed book? Check out www.abebooks.com for over 45 million titles of used, rare, first edition, and out of print books. You might just find the perfect novel to share as a host, or with your host!

Looking for cutting-edge conversation for your dinner party? My favorite stop on the information highway is www.fark.com, which constantly updates outrageous "strange but true" stories from around the world. From the inane ("Serial snuggler surrenders to police") to the asinine ("Bleeding statues turn out to have semi-rational explanation"), you'll find it there!

You can always count on 800-FLOWERS [356-9377] to come through when a plant or bouquet is needed. Personalized, seasonal floral arrangements are a great way to say thank-you if you've been invited to someone's dinner party. It's also a gracious way to send your regrets if you have to turn down the invitation. Their website, www.800flowers.com, features other unique specialty items.

Acknowledgments

Take note of these names. You might be lucky enough to one day have these talented people as guests at *your* dinner party!

For encouragement and support, my friends and mentors who teach so much by example: my awesome editor Jeremie; The Forbes family; Bonnie & Keith and the Hollywood Happy Hour gang; Gena & Pankaj; Pam & Oli & Jack; Tasha; Marita; Alexandra & Rob; Marie; Amy; Jane & Bob; Melanie & Lee; J.D.; everyone at Sunrise and GMTV, Heather & Pat; my agents Maura, Mark, & John; Boxx Communications; Carol Lynley; Jeff Werber; Dan; Jon; the late Mary Stuart; Terry; Danny; Jeff; Michael; Diana; The Brains & Brawn workout team; my marathon running group; the folks at Borders Books; Mali; Seth & Kylee; Marc & Carol; Heather & Peter; Maria; Elizabeth; Philece; Realtor Rick & Greg; Nancy; Peter & Andy; Neil; Zack; John; Bill; all my wonderful publicist pals, Stacey, Deb, & Lori; Mimi Kennedy; Natalie Raitano; Kathleen; Marcia; Mrs. Gibson; Mrs. Fryer; Traci; Lois & Henry for keeping me company every step of the way; my friends & family back East.

Cover photography by Michael Higgins (Reba McIntyre's hottest backup dancer and my talented lensman); caricatures by Philip Argent; couture by Cantu & Castillo and Charlie Lapson, who not only dress the stars, but make me feel like one every time I have their clothes on my back!

Way-y-y too many to mention! If I left anybody out, I owe you a dinner!

INDEX

ABOUT THE AUTHOR

Nelson Aspen is an entertainment and lifestyles reporter living in Los Angeles. A popular personality in TV, radio, and print, he is currently a Hollywood correspondent for the wildly popular morning shows of the United Kingdom, *GMTV*, and Australia, *Sunrise*. See? It really *is* accurate to say that millions of people have woken up with Nelson over the course of his career. He spent three successful seasons as the Los Angeles producer and presenter for *TV Guide Television*, and worked for diverse showbiz outlets, acquiring monikers that included "The Groovy Gossip Guy," "The TV Guide TV Guy" and "The Party Patrolman." His wide range of interviews spans from superstars like James Cameron and the late Bob Hope to plastic surgeons, personal trainers for pooches, and people who claim to "hypnotize your boobs or penis bigger" (it didn't work for him). You can also find him on the Web at www. nelsonaspen.com.